BECOMING
KAREEM

BECOMING
KAREEM

Growing Up On and Off the Court

BY **KAREEM ABDUL-JABBAR**
AND **RAYMOND OBSTFELD**

Ⓛ Ⓑ
LITTLE, BROWN AND COMPANY
NEW YORK BOSTON

Little, Brown and Company
Hachette Book Group
1290 Avenue of the Americas, New York, NY 10104
Visit us at LBYR.com

First Edition: November 2017

Little, Brown and Company is a division of Hachette Book Group, Inc.
The Little, Brown name and logo are trademarks of Hachette Book Group, Inc.

The publisher is not responsible for websites (or their content) that are not owned by the publisher.

Library of Congress Cataloging-in-Publication Data
Names: Abdul-Jabbar, Kareem, 1947- author. | Obstfeld, Raymond, 1952- editor.
Title: Becoming Kareem : growing up on and off the court / Kareem Abdul-Jabbar,
Raymond Obstfeld.
Description: New York : Little, Brown Books for Young Readers, 2017.
Identifiers: LCCN 2017036942 | ISBN 9780316555388 (hardback) |
ISBN 9780316555333 (ebook) | ISBN 9780316478137 (library edition ebook)
Subjects: LCSH: Abdul-Jabbar, Kareem, 1947– Juvenile literature. | Basketball players—
United States—Biography—Juvenile literature. | Social reformers—United States—Biography—
Juvenile literature. | BISAC: JUVENILE NONFICTION / Biography & Autobiography /
Sports & Recreation. | JUVENILE NONFICTION / Biography & Autobiography / Social
Activists. | JUVENILE NONFICTION / Sports & Recreation / Basketball. | JUVENILE
NONFICTION / Biography & Autobiography / Cultural Heritage. | JUVENILE
NONFICTION / History / United States / 20th Century. | JUVENILE NONFICTION /
Religion / Islam. | JUVENILE NONFICTION / Social Issues / Adolescence. | JUVENILE
NONFICTION / Social Issues / Prejudice & Racism.
Classification: LCC GV884.A24 A3 2017 | DDC 796.323092 [B]—dc23
LC record available at https://lccn.loc.gov/2017036942

ISBNs: 978-0-316-55538-8 (hardcover), 978-0-316-55533-3 (ebook)

Printed in the United States of America

LSC-H

10 9 8 7 6 5 4 3 2

*This is dedicated to all the young people who value
scholarship and the teachers and mentors who sacrifice for them.
I especially want to thank Dr. John Henrik Clarke
because the Harlem Youth Action Project, which he created,
was crucial to me in understanding my path.*

—KAJ

*This book about the journey to becoming who you want
to be is dedicated to my children, Max and Harper,
whose own journey has been a constant source to me
of wonder, appreciation, and inspiration.*

—RO

Every Kid Needs a Coach

The world knows me as Kareem Abdul-Jabbar.

I'm in the basketball record books under that name. I traveled the world as a US global cultural ambassador under that name. Google lists me about five hundred thousand times under that name. I was inducted into the Basketball Hall of Fame under that name. I received the Presidential Medal of Freedom from President Obama under that name. Part of that name has been passed on to my five children and to my grandchild.

But that wasn't the name I started life with, or grew up using. When I was a child, my friends and family knew me as Lewis Alcindor. Everyone called me Lew.

When I was twenty-four, I changed that. My team, the Milwaukee Bucks, had just won the National Basketball

Association (NBA) championship, and I had been voted the Finals' Most Valuable Player. Everything was going perfectly. The fans were cheering my name, Lew, and sports journalists were writing about how bright my future would be. I was at the height of the success I had worked so hard my whole life to achieve. Which is why it came as such a shock when the day after winning the national championship, I announced to the world that I was no longer Lew Alcindor, but Kareem Abdul-Jabbar, which means "noble servant of God."

The world responded: "Huh?"

Three years earlier, while still a college student at the University of California, Los Angeles (UCLA), I had quietly converted to Islam, which I had been studying for several years. People thought it was just a phase I was going through—an impressionable college kid experimenting with alternative ideas and lifestyles, like becoming a vegan or getting an eyebrow piercing. They figured that as soon as I signed a contract for major money with a professional basketball team, I would revert to my familiar former self. But by changing my name in such a high-profile way, I was announcing on a much grander scale that I was no longer Catholic, but Muslim. No longer Lew, but Kareem.

And that I had no intention of going back.

Because of my fame as a professional basketball player, and because so few Americans knew anything about Islam back in the 1970s, there was a lot of angry backlash. People did not want me messing with their idea of who I was or what I represented to them. To many, by changing my religion and name, I was no longer the *typical* American kid playing a *typical* American sport embodying *typical* American values. I had become something foreign and exotic, like a newly discovered species of tree frog that just might be poisonous.

To me, by changing my religion and name, I was embracing the American ideal of freedom even more than when I was Lew Alcindor. I was becoming the person I chose to be rather than the person everyone was trying to convince me I should be. Lew Alcindor carried the name and religion of the white slaveholder who had exploited, humiliated, and abused my ancestors. How could I allow my successes to honor the name of such a villain? Instead, I decided to adopt the name and religion of many of the Africans who had been kidnapped and sold into slavery. Those were the people I should be honoring.

But many who learned of my decision were furious. Reporters wrote nasty things, fans wrote outraged letters, and some people even threatened to kill me. My parents were shocked and hurt by my rejection of their name. My teammates were confused; some felt personally betrayed. Despite all that, I knew I had made the right choice because I was, after all those years, finally who I wanted to be.

The long road to discovering who I wanted to be was not straight or easy. I made mistakes—plenty of them. Fortunately, I didn't have to travel that road by myself. Sometimes it felt as if I were walking alone, carrying a heavy burden on my shoulders. But then I'd look up and see someone there to help me carry that weight, or to shine a light on the path ahead so I knew where to go and what to avoid. I didn't always realize they were helping me at the time, nor did I always listen to them. At least the mistakes were mine and the successes were mine because the path was mine.

From grammar school through my twenty years as a professional basketball player, my team coaches have helped guide me. But I have also had other people who helped me along my path even though they weren't part of any team. I think of them as life coaches. Some were teachers, like my martial arts teacher and an eventual international movie star, Bruce Lee. Some were friends, like the world champion boxer Muhammad Ali. Some were actual coaches, like my UCLA coach John Wooden, whose lessons on and off the court still deeply influence me today. Some were writers, singers, poets, athletes, or activists whom I never met, and who may have even lived hundreds of years ago, but whose lives and works inspired me to see the world differently and helped me see my place in it.

Those who loved me weren't always the best coaches. Some who thought they were providing guidance were actually negative influences—and I learned from listening to their words and watching how they behaved that I needed to do the opposite. That is one of the hardest lessons to learn. Good intentions don't always have good results.

We are all told what to do and what to think from the moment we are born. Early lessons are pretty easy: where to poop and pee, how to walk, keeping fingers out of blenders and electrical sockets. After that, things get trickier. Parents, siblings, friends, peers, teachers, governments, employers, political parties, media, and religions are all stuffing heavy bricks of their opinions into our mental backpack. Then they shove us out the door to stagger along the path under all that weight of expectation and pressure, without ever asking us if the path is what we truly want.

My journey from Lew Alcindor to Kareem Abdul-Jabbar was my quest to figure out what path *I* wanted. I often felt like Pinocchio dancing as someone else tugged my strings. But as I grew older, I realized that each choice I made was me cutting another string so I could move freely on my own. Only when I'd cut all the strings could I become the person I truly wanted to be and—more important—needed to be.

PART 1

What My Coaches Through Eighth Grade Taught Me

(Even When They Didn't Mean To)

_____

"You fail all the time,
but you aren't a failure until
you start blaming someone else."

FOOTBALL COACH BUM PHILLIPS

How I Discovered
I Was Black

I didn't realize I was black until third grade.

Although I was born in the predominantly black community of Harlem in 1947, I was raised in a multiethnic housing project in the Inwood section of Manhattan. Our project consisted of seven buildings, each fourteen stories tall, with twelve apartments on each floor. That totaled 1,176 apartments. Basically, a small, crowded city.

Our neighbors formed a mini United Nations of Russians, Scandinavians, Jews, Irish, Puerto Ricans, and Cubans, along with about 15 percent black residents. My friends and neighbors spoke in a variety of lilting and guttural accents, which thrilled me. To be exposed to so many different cultures and languages—and foods!—was so much more interesting to a curious little boy than everyone looking, talking, and acting the same.

That's not to say that everybody always got along, especially the kids. We had our share of bullies and mean kids. Because I was taller than almost everyone my age, most neighborhood children didn't challenge me. But I was a well-mannered, gentle child who regularly attended church in my Sunday suit and tie, with no desire to fight nor skills to win a fight. The hard-core bullies always seemed to know which kids, regardless of their size, didn't have any fight in them, so they zeroed in on me.

One girl, Cecilia, who was three years older, made me her pet project for beatings. She had no particular reason to dislike me—it was as if she picked on me as a form of exercise. More than once she chased me around the playground near our house. I'd try to outrun her but she was fast and relentless. She always caught me and then gave me a few extra punches for making her run.

Once, she chased me after Little League practice while I had my Louisville slugger in my hand. I still ran, but this time when she cornered me on that same playground, I took a couple of tentative swings with my bat at her legs. If

I'd actually hit her, I probably would have burst into tears, but that never happened. She sneered at my sad attempt at self-defense, snatched the bat from my hands, and shoved me to the ground. She straddled me and pressed the bat against my throat with a victorious smile. I flailed like an overturned beetle, afraid she would choke me to death, but eventually she hopped off and strolled away. I figured she didn't want to hurt me too badly or she wouldn't be able to chase me the next time.

Despite these typical kid conflicts, I was never picked on because of my race. Because the projects were filled with so many different ethnicities, no one risked casting the first stone. My mom and dad never talked about being black, and I was too young to know about the violent racial tensions going on throughout America at that time. It was the 1950s and the world was changing. As far as I knew, we were all the same.

My wake-up call came in third grade when my classmate Michael brought a Polaroid camera to school. Until the Polaroid, all cameras had a roll of film inside that had to be mailed away or taken to a special store to be developed. Sometimes you would wait weeks between the time you snapped a photo and the time you got to see what it looked like. The Polaroid, to our delight, spit out an "instant" photograph.

Giddy over this cool gadget, we decided to take a class photo. I attended a strict Catholic school, with students wearing traditional uniforms: boys in white shirts, blue ties, and navy blue slacks and girls in jumpers and knee socks. Our teacher arranged us by size in front of the blackboard, snapped the photo, then shooed us back to our seats while she removed the miracle image from the camera. The photo, still moist and smelling of sour chemicals, was passed around from student to student, each marveling at this breakthrough technology that, to us, could only mean that jetpacks and flying cars were merely months away.

But when the photo finally landed on my desk, I didn't see it as a tiny window into a space-age future. I just saw myself, as if for the first time. There I was, freakishly towering over all the other kids, with skin much darker than everyone else's.

Tilting the glossy photo in the harsh classroom light didn't change anything. I was still black.

And my classmates weren't.

I knew two other kids in my school, but not in my classroom, who were also black, but I hadn't seen myself as the same as them—yet not different from them, either. I just hadn't realized how different we looked from the other kids.

I didn't bring up this startling discovery with my parents. They had never mentioned it. No one at school had mentioned it. Maybe no one else noticed, or maybe it was supposed to be a secret. Maybe I had a secret identity, like Superman. Maybe my superpower just hadn't kicked in yet.

But the color of my skin wasn't quite the secret identity I thought it was. As we advanced through the grades, I didn't gain a superpower to protect me, and my skin made me more of a target. As every kid who has ever been a target in school knows, the best way to survive is to become invisible. To keep your head down, not make eye contact, not call any attention to yourself. It's not exactly a superpower, but it is a survival skill. However, for me, that was impossible. If my black skin made me a target, then my abnormal height made me a highly *visible* target, like a giraffe trying to hide among gerbils.

Realizing I was black didn't affect my life right away. I still had plenty of friends, most of them white. I was still the Lew who played occasional pranks at school, mostly slapstick stuff I saw the Three Stooges do on TV, like pulling out a chair when a kid was about to sit down, then saying, "Nyuk, nyuk, nyuk."

My best friend, Johnny, was white. Our mothers were close, so we had lots of opportunities to play together. We celebrated each other's birthdays together, hung out at school together, and played after school together. We were inseparable. Our specialty was building models of tanks, battleships, and fighter jets. We would sit for hours, gluing each tiny plastic propeller into place with the precision of brain surgeons. A typical conversation was arguing about which football and baseball players were best. Sometimes we sat in silence, concentrating on painting our models, just happy to be in each other's company.

We were also in Little League together and spent as much time as possible playing stickball with the other neighborhood kids. When we were together, no one picked on either of us because we had each other's back. They knew that even mild-mannered Lew wouldn't back down from a fight if anyone threatened Johnny. As far as both of us were concerned, we were each other's brother. Color didn't matter.

First Coaches: Mom and Dad Sang the Same Song

My parents were my first coaches. Together they had just one goal for Team Lewis Alcindor: Education! Education! and—say it with me—Education! My mom was especially fervent in preaching the gospel of education from her kitchen table pulpit. Her child was going to go to school every day, study hard, and get straight As. Nothing short of an alien invasion would get in the way. Even then, she'd be the one yanking slimy tentacles and reptilian tails from Martian bodies if they blocked my route to the school.

"Lewis, what are you doing?" she'd sometimes ask when she saw me being idle for too long.

"Nothing."

"Lots of kids are doing that. But somewhere there's a child doing extra schoolwork. That's the one you have to worry about."

I didn't understand why I had to worry about that kid, but I hit the books anyway.

Most parents in America want a good education for their children. They attend Open House Night, they help build crude models of plant cells, they constantly bring up college as an inevitable destination. But as important as education is to white middle-class and upper-class families, it's even more important to immigrant families, poor families, minority families. It's the only practical hope for them to get out of the cycle of poverty that many live in. Education is a life raft on a stormy, dark ocean.

I wasn't aware of this when I was a kid and my parents were nagging me to study, study, study. They offered cash incentives for good grades. A good report card meant doubling my allowance to one dollar! That was as far as their hands-on involvement went. If I had a question about my studies, my dad would silently point to a book on the shelf, end of discussion. My mom would just shrug. My parents taught me that education was the key to success, and they did their best to act as cheerleaders to my studies. But when it came to the actual day-to-day learning, I was on my own.

Fortunately, my default setting was Good Boy, which meant that I pretty much did whatever they told me. If they said study, I studied. If they said wash your hands, I washed my hands. I didn't whine or complain or talk about how other kids didn't have to study as much I did. I just said, "Yes, ma'am," or "Yes, sir," and got on with it.

I enjoyed reading and was always ahead of most other students at school. While the rest of my class was working on one story, I had already consumed three. I was an excellent student with great report cards. I guess I was the child other kids had to worry about.

But I was also reserved in class; I was anxious to please the teachers, so I could get good grades to please my parents. Because I was an only child, all my parents' focus was on me to succeed. Sometimes I wished I'd had a brother or sister so they could back off from pushing me so much. For my daily routine, I got up, went to school, came home, briefly played with the neighborhood kids, ate dinner, did my homework, watched an hour of TV, went to bed. Being the Good Boy wasn't exhausting work, but it was boringly predictable.

Coach Dad's Quiet Lessons

My mom was a seamstress at a large department store. My dad was a transit cop for New York City. They shared a love of music—and of being secretive around me.

As a child, I didn't think of my dad as secretive so much as just nonverbal. He didn't like to talk, as if each word he uttered cost him twenty hard-earned dollars. What he didn't understand was that each word he didn't utter cost our relationship a lot more. Days would pass without us talking. When I'd approach him with a problem, he'd react with a cool detachment, like a cop taking notes at a crime scene. Everything he didn't say that I needed him to say—whether words of advice or encouragement or love—pushed me further from him.

"Big Al," as he was called, was two hundred pounds and six foot three. He loomed over my childhood, casting a large, cold shadow. Others in the neighborhood were equally intimidated by his size and his general demeanor of intense judgment. He was the Punisher and Judge Dredd of the housing project.

My father was considered by many of his friends to be an intellectual because he read so much. Our house was filled with books and magazines, which he would buy, read, and sell back to the used-book store. But having such a well-read father didn't provide the advantage I'd hoped for. On the one hand, there were plenty of books around that helped me develop my own passion for reading, which has become one of the great joys of my life. On the other, my father used books like the Great Wall of China, to keep intruders out of his private kingdom. If I asked him a question, he'd hand me a book. If I persisted for a more personal response, he'd shoo me away, his book open wide in front of his face so he couldn't see me.

While he was in high school, when homes in poor neighborhoods still used real ice as refrigeration, he had a job hauling fifty-pound blocks of ice from wagons up flights of stairs. That's the image that most stayed with me through my life: my father as an iceman, as cold as the translucent, thick slabs he carried.

But my dad also had a secret identity: He wasn't just a cop, he was also an accomplished musician. He had a musicology degree from the Juilliard School of Music, one of the most prestigious music schools in the country. He played trombone with a lot of well-known jazz musicians, many of whom he introduced me to. He and my mom even sang together in the Hall Johnson Choir, a famous black choral ensemble that performed in Broadway shows and movies featuring African American spirituals. Music animated my father. When he was either playing music or dancing, he was smiling and happy. When he wasn't, it was as if someone had opened his valve and let all the air out. He sagged back into his easy chair, as lifeless as a deflated doll.

Dad was coaching me even when he didn't know it. His love of music, especially jazz by greats such as Miles Davis and Gil Evans, infected me, too. Even Big Al noticed my enthusiasm and asked me if I wanted to learn the trombone. He didn't offer to teach me on his own sacred instrument, of course, but if I wanted to take it up, a friend of his was selling one. The problem was, I didn't want to play the trombone, I wanted to play the tenor sax like my musical hero John

Coltrane. Dad knew I was interested in the sax, and that his musician friends had even offered to give me free lessons, but he never spoke of it. In the end, I abandoned the idea of becoming the next Coltrane because it took too much time and I wasn't getting any encouragement from home. And as far as Big Al was concerned, either I followed in his rigid footsteps or I was invisible.

For some fathers and sons, sports can be a bonding experience. Not so much for me and my dad.

Baseball was my first love, and I gleefully played Little League for four years, from the time I was eight to when I was twelve. My mom and dad came to a couple of Little League games during those four years, but it wasn't a priority. At least I won Player Having the Most Fun Award. That was a pretty accurate assessment of my sports skills.

One day, my father decided to play basketball with me. I imagined we were starting a new tradition of the two of us doing more things together. No more just pointing to books and grunting, or freezing me out in silence when I asked a question. Today was the start of a whole new father-son relationship. Soon we'd be chatting about our favorite athletes over breakfast.

It didn't happen.

In his determination to beat me, he threw his elbows into my ribs, shoved me out of his way, and knocked me around as if I were a tackling dummy. "This is how you protect the ball," he said, then elbowed me in the face. "You gonna let me drive on you like you're a mannequin?" he'd say, then shoulder me aside as he drove to the basket. I had hoped that he would patiently teach me, help me improve so he could be proud of me. That we'd laugh about my mistakes the way these father-son scenes played out on television and in movies. Instead, he had brutishly proved his point that he was the man of the house.

We never played again.

4

Coach Mom's Practical Lessons

My mom was a more reasonable coach, and from her I learned how to be pragmatic about daily life, especially about money. Mom controlled the household budget, and though she and my father often argued about finances, Mom always won because Dad had no clue how to budget, pay the bills on time, and make every dollar stretch. Years later, after my mom had died and I was taking care of my dad, I would save money for him just as she had done. Otherwise, he would have gambled it all away on lottery tickets and trips to Las Vegas.

She also introduced me to one of the most influential coaches in my life: movies. We went to the movies often, especially if the film starred William Holden, whom she had a crush on. At that time, Holden was in his early thirties, a handsome man who often played a lovable rogue, someone just out for himself at the start of the movie, but ending up doing the right thing. We sat through the exciting Holden war films like *Stalag 17* and *The Bridges at Toko-Ri*, as well as the sappy movies like *Sabrina* and *Picnic*. I didn't care as long as I had a bag of popcorn and a cold soda. Those hours we spent watching the movies flicker on the big screen in front of us brought us closer. It was as if we were sharing a secret life filled with adventure.

I especially loved Westerns, which was a little ironic because my mother was part Cherokee and the villains were often savage Indians. Plus, there weren't many black people shown, so we didn't have anyone our color to identify with. I didn't care. Westerns were a major part of movies and television when I was a kid. There were Westerns on TV every night of the week, and it seemed like a new theatrical release every weekend. One episode of a favorite Western TV show, *The Rifleman*, particularly affected me. The guest star was Sammy Davis Jr., a popular singer, dancer, and actor who was known for being part of Frank Sinatra's infamous bad-boy celebrity crew called the Rat Pack. I had seen Sammy on other shows, singing and dancing, but this was the first time I saw him in a Western, and it was the first time I saw any black man as a main character in a Western. At best, black people in Westerns carried baggage, held other characters' horses, or swept the saloon floor. But Sammy was a gunslinger. He fast-drew his gun from his holster, spun it around his fingers, threw it in the air, and caught it in mid-spin with his trigger finger. He threw a knife at a barn door, drawing and firing his gun as the knife flipped toward the door, so the knife stuck in the bullet hole he'd just made! What? A black man who could do all that?

I fell in love with Westerns not just because there was a lot of action, from gunfights to Indian attacks to train robberies, but because I loved the idea of a frontier where people from any background could start over with a clean slate and become who they wanted to be, not who everyone expected them to be. It appealed to that part of me that was frustrated with always being the polite, well-mannered, obedient Good Boy. I imagined myself living in a Western town, making my own choices about who I should be and what I would stand for. I'd wear the hat, I'd wear the gun, and I'd be a little bad from time to time.

My passion for Westerns didn't diminish as I grew older,

but increased because I started to read history books. I discovered that despite the all-white cowboys of movies and television I grew up on, nearly 25 percent of cowboys were black. Many were ex-slaves trying to start over as free men. I also found out about Bass Reeves, a former slave who became one of the best and most feared lawmen in the Old West (and some say is the basis for the Lone Ranger character). I read about the ruthless black outlaws, the fearless black stagecoach drivers, and the courageous Buffalo Soldiers, black members of the 24th and 25th Infantry regiments of the US Army, formed in 1866.

My passion for Westerns started out as a child's fantasy for adventure, but it evolved into a source of cultural pride as I discovered the extent to which African Americans contributed to the development of the Old West, the time in American history that some say most defines America's personality of fierce individualism. As much as the history books tried to erase black participation—and the movies and TV shows I loved followed that example—we were there, helping to build a mighty country out of wilderness. I didn't want anyone to forget that. As an adult, I began collecting memorabilia from the West, including various antique guns. I even have a buckskin cowboy outfit, custom-made to fit my seven-foot-two frame, and a buff cowboy hat that I've worn in parades. When I'm dressed in my cowboy outfit and waving to the crowds, I become a living reminder of the true American history of black cowboys that is rarely taught.

So I guess my mom sparked that passion in me to explore history, even if she didn't realize she was doing it.

Actually, most of my mom's lessons as a coach were inadvertent. She wasn't a reader, nor did she have much interest in what was going on in the world, even though it was one of the most exciting times in history: The civil rights movement was making waves. But Mom's focus was on protecting me from whatever was going on in the outside world. Even though I could talk with her more easily, I couldn't speak openly about my real thoughts because they would have frightened her. But we ate dinner in front of the TV, watching the evening news. This was how I learned about everything that was going on outside. But if I asked any questions, they were met with silence. My parents had faced racial discrimination all their lives, but now that people were raging against it, they seemed frightened of the change.

I was ten years old in 1957 when the Soviet Union launched Sputnik, the first artificial satellite to orbit Earth.

"Wow! Did you see that?" I asked. "They put a rocket ship in space."

"Communists," my dad said with a frown.

"Not our business," my mom said. "Eat."

Between her overprotectiveness and my father's remoteness, I felt imprisoned much of the time, but I was luckier than many other kids my age in that I had my own room. When my friends came over to play, they were often envious of my private bedroom because they had to share with one, two, or even more family members. My room wasn't just a source of pride; it was my Fortress of Solitude, like Superman's, only without all the alien technology.

My mom thought she was doing her motherly duty keeping me safe from the world outside on the streets. My father thought he was doing his fatherly duty providing a home, clothing, and food on the table. However, they didn't teach me about the most important thing: being black in a white world. I had no coping skills when it came to racism.

But I got a crash course in racism—not from my white schoolmates, but at the all-black boarding school my parents sent me to for fourth grade. My time there was perhaps the single most transformative year in my life for a long while.

I came back a very different little boy from the one they'd sent there.

5

Boarding School: Good Boy in a Bad Place

When I first saw Holy Providence Boarding School's red-tile roofs and endless archways, I thought of it as just another Catholic school masquerading as a tranquil abbey. It was run by devout Catholics, and that meant lots and lots of rules strictly enforced. I'd already done three years in Catholic school, so I was an old pro at pleasing authority. The only difference, I figured, was that forty boys also lived there. There would be no daily escape to my home, especially to the safety of my room. No hours spent alone pleasantly reading adventure stories. No privacy. Ever.

I soon discovered there was another difference: Most of the boys were sent to Holy Providence not because education was a priority, as in my house, but because they had behavioral problems. Teachers, authorities, even their own parents didn't want them around anymore.

It was a reform school designed to transform tough kids into model students.

I didn't need reforming. I was already the model of what the teachers wanted the other boys to be. My reading skills were so advanced that even though I was in fourth grade, the teachers asked me to read to the seventh graders. I had a large vocabulary, spoke without slang, pronounced words properly, paid attention in class, volunteered answers, and was impeccably polite. Everything I did made the teachers love me—and the rest of the students hate me.

I never knew why my parents decided to send me there. Was it cheaper than St. Jude School? Were they having marital problems? Did they want to expose me to more kids of my color? I didn't know, and they never felt it necessary to explain to a shy and bookish nine-year-old boy why he was being ripped from his comfortable home, friends, and school and shipped away to live with a bunch of menacing strangers.

My mother had once told me never to let myself be intimidated by others. Great lesson, except she forgot to teach me exactly how to do that. What specific steps do I take? My father was never intimidated—he was the one who intimidated others—but he taught me how to defend myself. He taught me the physical notions, but I didn't have the fire and aggressive demeanor that made those techniques actually work. I was nine years old but already five foot eight. In nature, animals always try to make themselves look bigger to scare away predators, but my height was no defense against kids who could recognize weakness when they saw it. And when they did, they instinctively knew to pounce and devour. The Catholic teachers may have taught us that the meek shall inherit the earth, but at Holy Providence the meek were force-fed the earth.

I first learned about prejudice against skin color by being on the receiving end—not from white people, but from the other black kids at my school. Their hatred of me, I soon realized, was more than the typical anger at a teacher's pet or Nerdy McGeekerson. Although we were all black, I didn't act or speak like the black kids they hung out with, but more like the white kids I grew up with. To them, I was an Oreo: a black kid who acted too white—black on the outside, white on the inside. Their resentment of more privileged white people, as well as of black people who tried to fit into white society by acting like them, focused on me.

Quickly, their hatred took on a physical expression.

The school bully was a burly kid named Sylvester, who was three years older than me in age, but centuries ahead in street smarts. He decided one day that it would be fun to toss his marbles out the dorm window and have his underlings chase after them. Between his loud cackling laughter and the cracking sound of marbles smacking cement, the teachers soon demanded an explanation. Ever the Good Boy who could not tell a lie and always honored authority, I told them the truth. They punished Sylvester, but he punished me much worse. The beating was savage, not just for having told on him, but for being the kind of kid who believed it was the right thing to do. For being a smart, straight-A student who would have the kind of opportunities he had no chance at. For being an Oreo.

The bruises healed, but I didn't. Something deep inside me had broken. It's an odd feeling to be among your own people for the first time and be afraid of them. It made me feel completely alone. I had been abandoned by my parents and rejected by the one group that I thought would welcome me because we at least looked the same. But we weren't the same at all. If I didn't belong with them, where did I belong? I didn't just feel lonely and isolated because I was at that school; I felt that way because I was afraid I didn't fit in anywhere outside the school, either.

But I adapted. I continued to excel at school, but I was less vocal now. I kept to myself, avoiding contact with the other boys because I never knew what I might say or do to set them off. Instead of making myself bigger to scare away predators, I adopted another animal kingdom tactic: invisibility. Silence was my camouflage.

Eventually, I found sanctuary. A place where I could hide out in safety.

The basketball court.

Basketball had never been my game. I was slow and clumsy, and my brutal experience with my father on the court did nothing to make me like it any better. But there wasn't much else to do at school, and the court was a place where I could be by myself.

I would have been happy just practicing free throws by myself for the whole year. The school, however, had other plans. Despite my ineptitude, I was still the second-tallest kid, which automatically put me on the school's basketball team.

I wish what happened next would have been like the movies I used to see with my mom on Saturday afternoons: The moment I joined the team and stepped on the court, I showed the whole school what a great player I was, and the bullies came after the game to apologize and announce to everyone else that from now on no one had better mess with me.

That didn't happen.

The games we played against other Catholic elementary schools were barely organized. It was like throwing a chew toy and watching a pack of puppies scramble after it. There was a lot of running up and down the court, hurling the ball in the general vicinity of the basket. I ran, too, but in a loping shuffle. Flailing spastically was my go-to move. When it came to shooting, I had a better chance sitting on the ball and hatching a unicorn than making the ball swish through the hoop.

Although I was taller than almost everyone else, I hadn't yet developed much control of my body. Most kids grow gradually, which allows them enough time to adjust. I grew in sudden spurts that didn't give me much time to feel comfortable.

One day, all that changed. I was in the middle of a game, shocked that I wasn't on the bench, where I could do the most good for the team. I was struggling with the dribble, which looked simple but suddenly felt as if I were juggling chainsaws. I knew I was near our basket, so all I had to do was get rid of the ball and let someone else screw up. But I couldn't find anyone open. I had my back to the basket, and a kid from the other team was riding me so close I thought he was going to throw a saddle on my back. With no one to pass to, and lacking the skills to drive to the hoop, I looked over my shoulder at the basket, which didn't seem as tiny and far away as usual. Then I did something I had never done before: With one hand, I looped the ball over both my shoulder and the defender. The ball arced high over everyone and curved toward the basket. My heart thumped with anticipation. Sweet glory was only two seconds away.

The ball banged off the rim and bounced away.

Rather than slink away in defeat and humiliation, I took the very same shot the next time I got the ball. With the very same results. No basket. But I didn't care. At nine years old, I had found the shot that made me feel like an athlete, that made me feel I was in control of this gangly body that so far had done nothing but isolate me from others. Now, for the first time, my body was not an enemy but an ally.

Unfortunately, that confidence didn't transfer to my daily life among the other students. I focused only on academics and keeping to myself, but even so I left myself open to attack.

And attack they did. Two weeks before the end of the term, I was jumped by two guys who proceeded to pummel me in the face and body.

"Not so tough, Alcindor," one of them taunted, punching me in the back.

"Think you're so smart," another grumbled, kicking me in the ribs.

"Don't give a crap how tall you are."

Bullies seem to have the same lines of dialogue no matter what their race or where they're from.

Finally, they ran off laughing, leaving me balled up in pain and humiliation. It was a fitting farewell from Holy Providence, which had been more like Hellish Providence. The school's mission was to teach us the ways of Christian fellowship, but instead it had taught me the ways of violence and pettiness. A small seed of doubt had been planted inside me: about the Christian teachings, about my parents' affection, about my place as an African American. I was confused by it all—and angry.

When my parents picked me up from school, they immediately commented on how I had changed. I was sullen, didn't smile, didn't talk. They were right, and I blamed them for the change. They were my parents, my life coaches, and they had yanked me out of my safe and happy home and thrown me into a lion's den without any explanation or skills to survive. Why would I ever trust them again?

But if not them, then who?

Back in Black:
A Brand-New Lew

I f before serving hard time at Holy Providence, I was
defined by my friendliness, my goofy sense of humor, and
my love of learning, afterward I was defined mainly by
two things: height and race.

I still had my love of learning—maybe even more than
before, because after my experience with the kids at Holy
Providence, I was very aware of what a life without educational opportunities might be like. But I'd also learned that
being black had a whole set of additional challenges. That
even if I hadn't seen myself as black before, that was how
other people saw me. And I needed to figure out how to
cope with that on a daily basis.

Before Holy Providence, my height had been a novelty: something to joke about, but not to take seriously. "How's the weather up there, Lew?" "Hey, we found Bigfoot!" If somebody couldn't reach a book off the top shelf, he'd send for me. But suddenly I was aware that my height could be a tool to distinguish me. I wasn't a good basketball player, but I could be. And if I became good enough, I'd earn the respect of others—even the ones who thought I was an Oreo.

I had to work this philosophy out on my own because I no longer had any coaches. Although my parents continued to push my education, I thought of them more as drill instructors than coaches. I knew they loved me, but they didn't understand me. I had come back from boarding school with a lot of anger toward them for abandoning me, rather than protecting me. Even though I had joyfully reconnected with my neighborhood friends, I couldn't reconnect with my parents.

Years later, I would read a poem called "This Be the Verse" by the British poet Philip Larkin about how parents sometimes mess up their kids:

> *They may not mean to, but they do.*
> *They fill you with the faults they had*
> *And add some extra, just for you.*

That's how it was for me and my parents. A quiet coexistence in which they kept their eyes on my distant future without ever seeing what was going on in the here and now.

I received a crash course in race when I returned to New York. Anxious to get back to a normal life with my school buddies, I quickly joined the Little League again. To get to the playing field, I had to bicycle through Good Shepherd Parish, which was all Irish. They were Catholics, just like me, but they were white. So when they saw me biking through their neighborhood in uniform with my baseball glove, they would chase after me hollering, "Nigger! Nigger!" To keep them at a distance, I would swing my bike chain like a lasso as I speed-pedaled through. Every day was like a *Mad Max* run. Black kids from my projects would go to the fields in a group, which made us too many to take on.

I couldn't help but wonder how they could worship at a Catholic church and receive the same Christian lessons on loving your neighbor that I got, yet be filled with such rage and hatred when they saw me. What was the point of attending church if you weren't going to follow the teachings? Wasn't Jesus the main coach for all of us? There seemed to be something broken in the church if this was how its followers behaved. I buried that heresy deep inside because good boys didn't question the church, but the seed was planted, and it kept growing bigger as I did the same.

My next bout with racism hit closer to home.

My best friend, Johnny, and I hadn't communicated during my year away. There were no cell phones, texting, or e-mails then, so all communication had to be through letters. At nine years old, dutifully writing to my parents was all that I could handle. But when I returned, Johnny and I picked up our friendship again pretty much the same as before I'd left. After a year without any close friends, I was relieved to see his smiling face and feel his hearty slap on my back followed by, "So, where've ya been, Lew?"

"Hunting big game in Africa. What about you?"

"You know, keeping the neighborhood from falling apart without you."

We settled back into our routine of games, models, and arguing about sports.

Johnny and I still played sandlot football with other neighborhood kids and rode our bikes together. When the boxing champion Sugar Ray Robinson drove through our neighborhood on the way to his mother's house in Riverdale, Johnny and I would run along the sidewalk waving and shouting, "Hey, Sugar Ray!"

We were still best friends.

That summer, we went to St. Jude's day camp together. As a special treat, the camp counselors took us to George Washington High School, which had a swimming pool. Johnny's little sister was there, but we ignored her while concentrating on splashing each other in the pool. Then I noticed that she had disappeared. I was ten, but I was tall enough to see her quietly drowning at the bottom of the pool, surrounded by laughing and splashing kids. I quickly waded over to her, snatched her up by the arms, and dragged her to the side of the pool. She coughed up some pool water, but otherwise she was okay. "Jeez, Lew, you saved her life," Johnny said, his eyes brimming with tears. "I guess," I said. I didn't want to make a big deal of it. We were best friends, and best friends looked out for each other. But Johnny continued to pat me on the back and thank me. He was so grateful that I was sure our friendship had been cemented for life.

Then, in sixth grade, Johnny and I started to drift apart. I didn't see him as often after school. We didn't hang out in my room. We didn't build models or discuss sports. After a while, we barely nodded to each other in the hallway. He'd taken to hanging out with his white friends, without inviting me to join them. At first, I didn't know what was happening. I tried talking to him, but he was brusque and dismissive, assuring me nothing was wrong, but always having to hurry off to be somewhere else. Somewhere I wasn't. The pre–Holy Providence Lew Alcindor would probably have pestered him for some sort of explanation, maybe even asked his sister or parents, but the post–Holy Providence Lew was made of tougher stuff. If he didn't want to be my friend, then fine.

Around this time, St. Jude added two more black kids to the school population, and the three of us gravitated to one another, which was only natural given the undercurrent of racial hostility that was evident to us, even when it wasn't evident to the white kids. The three of us trudged through the halls of school every day with that burden saddled on our backs.

One day in seventh grade, Johnny started a fight with me. We were in the lunchroom, and I was kidding around with a pal of mine who was sitting next to Johnny.

"Hey, man," I said, "you watch *Twilight Zone* last night?"

"Yeah," he said, "the one with the alien who looks like you?"

I laughed. "The aliens looked like humans, which leaves you out."

Brilliant twelve-year-old humor.

"Leave me, earthling," he said, giving me a playful shove.

"Not until I destroy all alien invaders!" I gave him a little shove to the shoulder.

The shove knocked him into Johnny, who had been ignoring us. A couple of years earlier, he and I would have had this same kind of conversation about a favorite show. Not anymore.

Johnny jumped up and spun around. "Quit shoving, Alcindor!" And he swung at my head.

He must have been remembering the skinny, weak Lew he knew before Holy Providence. But this Lew was more than six feet tall and wasn't afraid of being punched. The fight ended with his getting a bloody nose and both of us being sent to the principal's office. My dad was called in, but when he arrived and was told what had happened, he was just annoyed at having his time wasted. This was a perfect coachable moment for his son, but he was too busy to express moral outrage or seek social justice or even just comfort his son. Instead, he left while Johnny and I sat in the principal's office until the end of the school day. When I walked out of school, Johnny and his pals were waiting for me. They taunted me with the usual insults: "Hey, jungle bunny! You big jungle nigger!"

The words hurt worse than the fight. We could always

get over a physical fight and be friends again, but words opened up a bottomless pit that could never be crossed. Seeing the same boy I used to laugh with in my room, celebrate birthdays with, swap models with, now standing there, his face contorted in hate while screaming at me, ignited a fire inside me that burned away our friendship forever.

Those were the last words I ever heard from my former best friend. We never spoke again, and his family moved away the following year.

I had lost more than my best friend. I lost my default trust in white people. I still had white friends at school, and would continue to have many close white friends throughout my life, but that day made me warier, more suspicious, when a white person offered friendship. I had to ask myself each time whether that same person laughing and joking with me now would one day stand in front of me shouting "Nigger!" in my face.

7

I, Basketball

The coaching I wasn't getting at home I finally started getting at school. Coach Farrell Hopkins, the athletics director, was a kind man who made sure I knew that no matter how I played, I was a valuable member of the basketball team—and a valuable human being. Coach Hopkins didn't single me out for special treatment; he was that supportive of all the boys. To see someone that caring in an atmosphere where most teachers seemed to be dispassionately doing their jobs was inspirational to me. I tried harder to be worthy of his confidence.

I spent much of fifth and sixth grade riding the bench. Even so, Coach Hopkins saw something in me and asked George Hejduk, a college boy from the neighborhood who occasionally assisted Coach Hopkins, to help me. George started teaching me the Mikan Drill, which involved shooting the ball with the right hand off the backboard, catching it with both hands, and then shooting with the left hand, catching it with both hands, and repeating back and forth.

That shot, the hook shot, was not new to me; I first used it at Holy Providence. One of the greatest practitioners of the hook shot was the NBA Hall of Famer George Mikan (whose drill I was being taught), who used it to crush team after team while playing for DePaul University in the mid-1940s. Later, in high school and college and as a professional player, my hook shot stood out because I did it from farther away, and with a much higher arc, which made it difficult to block. The radio broadcaster Eddie Doucette described the arc as "so high that it was coming out of the sky." That's how my shot became famous as "the Skyhook."

Thanks to the shot I stumbled into that day in fourth grade, as a professional basketball player I was able to set the NBA record for the most career points scored: 38,387, an average of 24.6 points per game. That total-points record still stands, though I'm sure there's some spunky nine-year-old somewhere right now practicing a new shot who will beat my record. I hope so. Because a coaching lesson that I would want to pass on to him or her is that records are merely steps on a ladder to help the next person move higher. All I did was hammer a new step on that ladder, setting a goal to inspire the next player.

As a result, by seventh grade, I was a pretty decent player. I was no longer an XXL benchwarmer, I was a force in the game. That year, we received new uniforms and I was allowed to choose my own number. I picked 33 because my favorite sports hero then, the New York Giants fullback Mel Triplett, also wore 33. He'd scored the opening touchdown in the 1956 championship game that the Giants won against the Chicago Bears, and I couldn't help but feel a surge of pride that he was black. He moved with power and grace and had the serious look of a man you didn't want to mess with. That was the kind of man I wanted to be, so 33 became my number from seventh grade until I retired from the NBA thirty years later.

Through basketball, I found my superpower. My power wasn't in being a great player, but in loving something enough to work hard at being better. I had a passion for playing, and that passion powered me like a generator. I discovered I had some small scraps of power and grace like my hero Mel Triplett. I discovered I could work together with other players to form a bond as a team. I discovered I was eager to learn more about how to improve. I discovered that it didn't matter whether I was a great ballplayer at that moment because I could become one if I worked hard enough. Who I was and who I would become didn't depend on my parents or on others who yelled insults at me. It depended on my own determination and discipline.

With that in mind, I spent the summer before eighth grade practicing my new move, the slam dunk. Because the basketball hoop is ten feet off the ground, most people will never know the exhilarating feeling of leaping above the rim and jamming the ball through with a clang from the rim, cheers from the crowd, and the glare of frustration on the other team's faces. The slam dunk was relatively new at this time. The seven-foot center and Olympic gold medalist Bob Kurland was dunking in the 1940s and 1950s, but it wasn't common practice. Teams that got dunked on took it personally, and they would retaliate against the dunker by running into his legs while he was in the air. That would cause the player to crash into the hard floor, sometimes resulting in serious injury that would remove him from the game.

I was aware of all that, but by eighth grade I was six foot eight, and I was determined to leave my mark on the game.

I got the chance during one game when my teammate

stole the ball at half-court, bounce-passed it to me, and I leaped up high above all the other players and slammed the ball through the hoop as if I'd been doing it all my life. The sixty or so spectators jumped to their feet, screaming and clapping.

When that ball went through the hoop, it was as if I'd followed it, like Alice in Wonderland falling down the rabbit hole into a strange new world.

I felt unstoppable.

Catholic high schools had started recruiting me before that, while I was still in seventh grade and a mere six foot five. I even had an offer from a private prep school, the Hill School in Pottstown, Pennsylvania. I would be the first black student attending. But I'd had enough of boarding schools, and I certainly didn't want the pressure of being the only black student. I could have my pick of any Catholic school in New York City, so why put myself through that kind of emotional pain?

In seventh grade, an older friend and teammate of mine was being recruited by Power Memorial Academy, a Catholic school in downtown Manhattan. Because the school had also contacted me, I decided to tag along with my friend to check the place out. It had a great academic reputation, so I knew my parents would be pleased. Academics were still important to me, too, but I was starting to get the feeling from all the attention by high school recruiters that this whole basketball thing was going to open a lot more doors for me than my good grades. So, as much as I appreciated its scholastics, it was the school's gymnasium and basketball coach that most interested me.

The gym didn't disappoint. It had a full court with six side baskets. Plus, it was open on Saturdays all winter, so I could practice as long as I wanted.

I didn't meet Coach Jack Donahue until eighth grade, when I was closer to having to make my decision. My friend took me to Power to shoot, and Coach Donahue was there. I liked him right away. He knew how to talk to kids my age: straight, as if their opinions mattered, but with humor. He didn't make exaggerated promises or try to flatter me. We just spoke basketball like two fans who loved the game. He even gave me and my friend passes to Madison Square Garden to watch the Knicks play.

I already felt alone at St. Jude. The civil rights tensions that were increasing on the streets outside seeped through our school walls, and my black face wasn't just Lew whom they'd grown up with, it was the face of the Negro Uprising that they overheard their parents fretting about or news commentators warning against. There was nothing aggressive from them, no name-calling as I'd had from Johnny, but the temperature between me and the white students, even my old friends, had cooled considerably. No one knew what to say or do, so we said nothing and did nothing. We still nodded in passing in the hallway, whispered to one another before class, chatted about *Twilight Zone* and *Have Gun— Will Travel* episodes, but everything was suddenly very polite and formal.

That made Power Memorial all the more attractive. A place to start over with a new team and a new coach. A place where they'd gone out of their way to welcome me. A student body that would see me as a sports hero, not just a black face.

As it turned out, Power Memorial Academy became the place of my greatest triumph—and greatest betrayal.

PART 2

High School Confidential:

New Heights in Basketball and Political Awareness

"I feel like a man who has been asleep somewhat and under someone else's control. I feel what I'm thinking and saying is now for myself."

MALCOLM X

8

Fresh Start, Fresh Problems

When I started high school, I was fourteen years old and six foot ten. The scary thing about being so tall when you're so young is that people automatically treat you as if you're older. Size implies maturity. Yes, I was the size of an adult (actually, bigger than most!), but I was still just a kid. And acting more like an adult wouldn't win me any friends. As a card-carrying Good Boy, I wanted to meet adults' expectations and get their praise, but as a Regular Kid, I wanted to be like my peers and get their friendship.

Welcome to high school, Lew.

Power Memorial Academy was a ten-story brick building that had once been a children's hospital, and it looked like a bleak institution. When I started attending in 1961, the school was already thirty years old, founded by a new community of the Christian Brothers of Ireland who had been invited to New York by Monsignor James W. Power much earlier. The inside was antiseptically clean, as befits the "cleanliness is next to godliness" belief of the Catholic administrators who ran it, but the building itself was already aging poorly.

As a bright and shiny freshman, though, all I cared about was the gym, and that had already received my stamp of approval. If we'd had Yelp back then, I would have given it an enthusiastic five stars just for the smell alone. That sounds gross to most people, but gym rats around the world know what I'm talking about. When you spend so many hours at a gym practicing, walking into it smells like home, whatever that smell is to each person. To me, it was fresh-baked sourdough bread, the aroma of hard work and camaraderie. The wooden floor gleamed under the shiny coats of varnish applied over the years. The bright overhead lights lit the room up like a stage.

I walked into school that first day resplendent in my blue blazer and slacks, the school uniform. We all looked like baby-faced accountants in training. I noticed some of my old classmates from St. Jude, the ones who had turned their backs on me, and we continued our policy of actively ignoring one another. I felt the pain of their betrayal, but I forced my face to remain expressionless. I couldn't let them see that they had hurt me. I shoved the pain deep down into the coldest part of my heart. I was here to study hard at academics and to work hard at basketball under my new coach, Jack Donahue. I was here to excel. Nothing else mattered.

I did excel. I made the honor roll my first semester, pleasing my parents and teachers. Learning came naturally to me. I loved reading, especially about history and adventure stories like *The Three Musketeers*. Basketball, however, I had to work at to do well in. But the fierce competitor that had been awakened in me loved challenges.

There was another awakening happening. Something deep inside that others couldn't see, but that was changing me as radically as my height.

During my freshman year at Power Memorial, the civil rights movement was picking up serious momentum. Every day, televisions blared stories of social unrest throughout the country. I would watch them during dinner with my mute parents as my insides filled with rage at the injustices against black people around the country—an injustice I felt only a small portion of by being snubbed by my white former friends. I followed every story the way an explorer follows a treasure map, hoping to discover the source of all my personal problems at school. Why had so many of the friends I grew up with suddenly turned against me? Why did the color of my skin offend—or scare—them so much? I soon learned that my little problems were just a tiny bit of the mountainous upheaval pushing through the streets outside.

In the southern part of the country, black people were still being forcibly segregated from white ones. That meant that people who were white had access to the best schools, shops, restaurants, and jobs, while those who were black were confined to dumpster diving for scraps. However, as the protest singer Bob Dylan observed, the times, they were a-changin'. In the year or so before I entered high school, black students had staged a sit-in at a "whites only" Woolworth's lunch counter in North Carolina, the US Supreme Court had outlawed the segregation of bus terminals throughout the country, and the University of Georgia had been ordered by a federal judge to desegregate. A group of white and black people called Freedom Riders traveled through the South to make sure the federal rulings against segregation of buses were being enforced. Although they encountered some violence and arrests elsewhere in the South, it wasn't until they arrived in Anniston and Birmingham, Alabama, that they got a taste of how deep racial hatred went.

On May 14, 1961, not long before the start of my freshman year, two buses containing Freedom Riders were attacked by a mob of Ku Klux Klan members, some of whom had come straight from church. One bus was stopped and firebombed, with Klan members holding the doors closed in an effort to burn the Riders, many young college students, to death. A gunshot or exploding fuel tank sent the Klan scurrying away, and the Riders were able to get out. The mob immediately jumped on the terrified Riders and beat them. As the Klansmen were about to lynch the battered students, highway patrolmen fired warning shots in the air, stopping them. The injured Riders were taken to a local hospital but were refused care.

When the second bus arrived in Birmingham, it was immediately attacked by the Klan, with the help of the local police. The Riders were beaten with baseball bats, iron pipes, and bicycle chains. The white Freedom Riders received the worst of the beatings because the Klan and the cops considered them to be "race traitors."

Events like these were what was going on in the world

outside our sheltered brick school. To the white students, it might have seemed like a few troublemakers not acting like patriotic Americans. But I was starting to see that these "troublemakers" were actually the patriotic ones, fighting for the rights everyone was supposed to have under the US Constitution we'd been studying so hard in class.

"I don't get what they're complaining about," my friend Mario said to me one day at lunch. I'd heard that before from my white classmates.

"Injustice," I said. "They want the same rights as white people have. That's the law."

"If it's already the law, then what's the big deal?"

"Not everybody follows the law," I said. "Or they find ways around it. Like using literacy tests to keep black people from voting."

Mario shrugged. "Maybe it's a good idea to make sure people can read before letting them vote. Otherwise, how can they know about issues?"

I shook my head in frustration. "Isn't your family from Italy?" With a last name like D'Angelo, I knew the answer.

"So?" he said, squaring his shoulders. In some neighborhoods, asking a kid where his family was from was the opening move for a fistfight.

"So," I said, "those literacy tests were originally started in the 1890s to keep immigrants from Russia, Italy, and eastern European countries from voting. If they couldn't read English, why should they have a say?"

I was right. My logic was sound. Yet I could tell by looking at his face that not only hadn't I changed his mind, but by angering him I might have hardened his opinion. I realized right then that changing people's minds wasn't just a matter of being right or offering evidence. I didn't know what to do about that, which made me feel helpless and useless.

Considering everything momentous that was going on outside, high school felt more and more like a protective bubble, and I felt as if I were living in a bubble within that bubble. I was isolated from most of the white kids, partly because of their attitude toward me, but also because of my own cautiousness. I'd been hurt enough times to be wary of people, and that icy wariness could have been as much a barrier as my skin color. I was discovering that racism was like a disease, and one of the side effects was that it made the victims withdraw from anyone who looked like the victimizers. All I knew was that I didn't want to have another friend like Johnny yelling, "Nigger!" at me ever again.

As much as I was isolated inside the school, I was also

isolated from the world-changing movement marching outside. I talked a big game in school, but what was I *doing* to change things? When I read the newspaper accounts of these important civil rights events, I couldn't help but notice how many were the result of student activists. Kids not much older than me were risking their lives to make the world better. They were out in the real world doing real things that made a difference. And I was dribbling a ball, winning games for the glory of a mostly white Christian school. I was too young to go out and do anything important, but my brain was starting to ask a lot of questions about who I was and the world I lived in.

Where, exactly, did I fit in?

One question that bothered me was how so many people could claim to be devout Christians, yet still justify the brutality they committed against black people. Not only the physical violence, but the daily harassment, humiliation, and indifference. To me, it seemed that every good Christian should be marching in the streets alongside the Reverend Dr. Martin Luther King Jr. until everyone was treated equally. Isn't that what Jesus would do? As far as I knew, the two people who most embodied Jesus's teachings were Mahatma Gandhi and Dr. King. One was a brown man from India who defeated the British Empire through nonviolent pro-tests, and the other was a black man from America who also led nonviolent protests. I wondered whether the only people who truly followed Jesus were those who were oppressed, the way the Jews, including Rabbi Jesus, were oppressed by the Romans.

I also couldn't understand why in history class, which was my favorite, we never read anything about the achieve-ments or accomplishments of anyone black. Yes, there was always a paragraph or two about George Washington Carver and how he invented peanut butter. The problem was that he did so many other wonderful things we never learned about...*and he didn't actually invent peanut butter.* The Aztecs had made peanut butter in the 1400s, and the patent for pea-nut butter in the United States was given to a Canadian phar-macist in 1884, twelve years before Carver began his tenure as head of the agriculture department at Tuskegee Institute. What other black scientists were we not hearing about? What about the black artists, poets, writers, musicians? Why had we never been taught that Alexandre Dumas, the author of my beloved *Three Musketeers* and *Count of Monte Cristo,* had been part black?

When I looked around at the white students in class as

we learned about the wonderful accomplishments of white people without ever hearing anything about black people, I could understand how these kids might find it difficult to believe that black people were their intellectual equals. That's what they were being taught. Worse, that's what I was being taught.

9.

Coach Donahue
to the Rescue—Sort Of

My refuge from the explosive turmoil outside, and the implosive turmoil I had started to feel inside, was basketball. The practices were so exhausting that I barely had time to think about anything else. Every school day I crawled out of bed early, went to school, practiced basketball until five o'clock, staggered home, powered through my homework, zoned out in front of the TV, and went to bed.

Weekends I hung out with my only close friend left in the projects, Norbert. We would shut ourselves in my room to play chess and talk about our plans for the future. He was determined to become a draftsman, making detailed drawings for engineers who were inventing wonderful new machines. I was going to be an architect and create futuristic buildings like the ones we saw on the TV show *The Jetsons*.

Because the civil rights movement was in the news every day, both of us had started to take an interest in finding out more about our ethnic origins.

"You know, we invented the yo-yo," Norbert, who was part Filipino, bragged one day in my room.

"Who's we?" I joked. "Your family? Cuz all I noticed you guys invented was the stench from cooking oxtails and plantain." I loved giving my buddy a hard time.

He ignored my jab. "Pedro Flores came to the United States from the Philippines, went to law school, dropped out, and invented the yo-yo."

Then I'd put on the latest jazz album by Sonny Rollins and say, "Yeah, but we invented that."

And back and forth we'd go, trying to one-up the other in a cultural heritage version of rock, paper, scissors. This kind of competition required that we do research. We even took the subway to the Metropolitan Museum of Art to find out more about Filipino and African cultures. Most important, I had a friend in whom I could confide any thought or feeling, knowing he would never make fun of me.

The demands of high school cut into the time I could

spend with Norbert. I had the studying part down, but the basketball part was as rocky as ever. As a freshman, my style of play reflected my personality: politely passive. I had some skills, but I didn't have an aggressive nature. The good players around me knew how to play rough, use their bodies with authority, and power their way to a rebound. I felt like a pinball bouncing off players rather than making them bounce off me. I knew I had to toughen up, and I was committed to getting better, but it wasn't happening fast enough.

Despite my size, my age and skill level meant that I practiced with the junior varsity team under Coach Dick Percudani, not Coach Donahue, who was the varsity coach. We played practice games against the varsity squad, which only highlighted my faults. They played with confidence and authority, snapping passes, running smooth plays, taking calculated shots. For me to ever play varsity seemed as far away a possibility as a black person becoming president.

On the morning our varsity team was scheduled to play a preconference game against Erasmus Hall High School in Brooklyn, Coach Donahue surprised me by taking me into his office. I figured he was going to discuss his disappointment in my progress as a player, maybe even say something about it all being a big mistake. That I didn't belong here. Instead, he handed me a varsity uniform.

"You'll be suiting up against Erasmus today," he told me.

I just stood there, the folded uniform in my hand. Was this a joke?

"Don't you have a class to go to?" he asked. He pretended to be all business, but I could tell by the slight grin he was enjoying my dumbfounded reaction.

When I unfolded the jersey, I saw the number 33—the one I had picked in seventh grade to honor the football player Mel Triplett. Even my fear of playing poorly and letting everyone down couldn't overcome my pride at walking out of his office with that uniform. I had no idea that would be the number I would wear for the rest of my basketball career. I hurried away on a mission to tell anyone who would listen that I would be playing varsity that afternoon. All day, as I sat in classes and walked the hallways and ate lunch, I allowed myself to imagine the game and the parts where I scored impossible shots, made incredible passes, snagged rebounds like a machine. Would the team insist on carrying me out of the gym on their shoulders or just award me the game ball?

Neither. We got slaughtered. Afterward, I sat in the locker room and cried.

I wish I could say I learned a great spiritual lesson from that day. Something clever and deep. But I didn't. I just felt as if I'd let everyone down—the team, my parents, the coach, the school. In the back of my mind, a voice scoffed, "Maybe you aren't as good as those white players."

That same month, we played Brooklyn's Abraham Lincoln High School as another tune-up before our league started. This time, I really tried to be a strong force, using my body and strength to claim my space on the court. But their seven-foot center was bigger and stronger and more experienced. He kept me out of the game to the point that I ended up fouling a lot out of desperation. After our loss, I didn't cry. I stormed around in frustration until Coach Donahue took me aside and said sternly, "I hope you're learning what it's like to really want to win."

What did that mean? I *had* wanted to win. I just didn't have the skills yet. Or the bulk.

Or did he mean something else?

I hadn't had any experience with a strong coach before. Until then, my coaches were standard-issue, one-size-fits-all men who were either nice guys who pushed sportsmanship more than winning or teachers picking up a few extra bucks to coach. Coach Donahue was different. Every game was personal to him, and he wanted it to be personal to us. Every win was an endorsement of our character, our will, our worth, and every loss revealed our faults, our weaknesses, our lack of commitment.

One reason Coach Donahue was so effective was that he was only thirty years old, younger than our parents, but old enough that he had that big-brother aura. A demanding big brother whom we all were desperate to please. When you did what he wanted and were successful, he heaped praise and love on you that would burn for days. When you didn't do what he wanted and failed, he would heap verbal abuse on you that would leave you feeling shriveled and worthless. He was like the US Marine drill sergeant in war movies who would lean into some frightened recruit's face, call him "Maggot!" and ask if he wanted to go home to Mommy. That coaching style drove us to do everything in our power to get his approval and avoid his insults. Basking in his warmth was much better than shivering in his cold.

We endured the cold with the heat because Coach Donahue knew how to win. He had been at Power Memorial for only a couple of years but had already posted an impressive win record, and we all wanted to take that record to new heights.

I especially wanted to win. I wanted to prove something both to myself and to white kids at the school. The racism being fought on the streets was both angering and inspiring. There were laws and politicians and violent mobs trying to make us feel as if we were lesser people. In my own class-rooms, a subtler racism was at work, telling us that we had never accomplished anything and that we never would. I was surrounded by teachers and students who believed that. I wasn't a Freedom Rider or marching with Dr. King or sit-ting at an all-white lunch counter, but I was competing. This was how I would help the cause.

But wanting to prove something and actually doing it were two very different things, especially when you're only fourteen.

"What are you, a stiff?" Coach Donahue would yell at me when I flubbed another rebound in practice. The rest of the team would stop to watch my embarrassment, grinning because this time it wasn't them. "Are you alive?" He'd grab my wrist and check his watch as if feeling for a pulse. "What are you, a farmer?" More laughter. "We play basketball here, Lew, not plow fields behind an ox. An ox would be faster than you right now."

And so on.

We were young enough to believe that all that mattered was results. If the coaching method made us winners, we wouldn't question whether there was a better, more effective way to achieve that goal. Besides, we all knew that his personal jibes weren't really personal—they came from a place of affection. Deep down, he cared about us. I was certain.

And because I was certain that he cared, I gave him my best.

In my first home game of league play, I was the starting center. I was fourteen years old and six foot eleven, but as thin as Jack Skellington in *The Nightmare Before Christmas*. Yet there I was, banging against older, heavier, rougher kids. After we won, one of the teachers came up and complimented me on how calm I looked through the whole game. "You drink ice water or something?" he asked. Truth was, my game face of fierce indifference had been developed off the court first. Interacting every day at the boarding school with tough kids looking to fight me, with white ex-friends at Power who blamed me for uppity black people demanding their civil rights, with white teachers ignorant of anything positive about black culture, had carved that stony Mount Rushmore game face. It was the only face I could have and survive.

Being fourteen was an especially important age to me because I was the same age as Emmett Till, the boy who had been haunting me since I was ten years old. Emmett was fourteen years old in the summer of 1955, when he traveled from his home in Chicago to visit relatives in Mississippi. Unaware of the harsh realities of Southern racism, Emmett was within the same vicinity as a twenty-one-year-old white woman who subsequently told her husband little Emmett had been flirting with her. Enraged, the husband and his half brother kidnapped Emmett that night, beat him, shot him, and dumped his body in the river. Both men were acquitted of kidnapping and murder, and because they were now safe from prosecution, they admitted to the crimes in an interview with *Look* magazine. (In a 2008 interview—made public nearly a decade later—Carolyn Bryant Donham, the white woman who accused Emmett of making advances to her that sparked his murder, confessed to lying and admitted that Emmett never approached her. In late December 2016, President Obama signed the Emmett Till Civil Rights Crimes Reauthorization Act of 2016, which encourages federal law enforcement agencies such as the FBI to continue to pursue civil rights cold cases.)

I was eight years old at the time of his murder but didn't

read about it until I was ten. It profoundly affected my sense of security in the world. Once I realized that a person, even a child, could be tortured and murdered just for being black, I no longer felt safe in my skin. Being black meant being a target. And the fact that two white men got away with it, and could brag about that in a national magazine, meant that the country didn't value our lives the way they valued the lives of white torturers and murderers of children. No one—not my parents, teachers, or friends—could explain how such a thing could happen in America. And now I was Emmett's age.

So, yeah, I had an impenetrable game face—to hide my fear on the court and off the court.

That game face, like the jersey number 33, followed me throughout my basketball career. It was a shield to protect me both on and off the court, and sometimes it got in the way of my getting to know people. I started to understand my father's hard and crusty exterior. I knew he'd always wanted to play in a symphony orchestra but wasn't able to because he was black. I now understood how that exterior could sometimes seep inside and fossilize until there's nothing left but hard and crusty.

We lost six games in my freshman season, but not for lack

of my effort. Colleges were already asking me to visit their campuses. Knowing that I was guaranteed a college education took a load off my shoulders and pleased my parents. That allowed me to concentrate even harder on improving my game. Coach Donahue emphasized working as a team, with no one showing off or trying to prove he was better than everyone else. He wanted a team, not superstars.

Yet one day during practice, in a moment of spontaneous whimsy, I fired off a turnaround jump shot that banked smoothly through the hoop. I'd seen Wilt Chamberlain do that same shot a hundred times, even at one of the games Coach Donahue took me to at Madison Square Garden, and wanted to try it for myself. But as soon as I hit that shot, Coach blew his whistle and stopped practice. "Look where you are," he said. "You're nowhere near the basket and shooting a low-percentage shot." To make his point of how absurd and selfish my shot was, he told me to shoot the same shot again. I did and it went in. "Shoot again," he demanded. It went in again. It went in six out of the seven times I shot it. "Yeah, you can make it in practice when no one's guarding you," he said with a scowl, "but don't try it in the game."

That got me thinking. He was right, of course, about its being a low-percentage shot in general. Therefore, it wasn't the best choice to make for the sake of the team. And I was nothing if not a team player.

But...

I couldn't help but also wonder when it was okay for a player to do something innovative, to try to push himself to a new level. Coach was right that there was a difference between how a player performs in the relative ease of practice and the high pressure of an actual game. Plays that were run flawlessly during practice could crumble when facing real opponents with practiced plays of their own. And I've seen really good players try to be a one-man team, scoring a lot of points in a losing game because they didn't involve the rest of the team. I didn't want to be the kind of player who racked up impressive stats for himself but caused his team to lose.

But I knew from my history studies that the biggest leaps in civilization are when individuals do something different and we all benefit from it. Galileo said the sun, not the Earth, was the center of our solar system, and they placed him under house arrest for the rest of his life because he wasn't being a team player with the Roman Catholic Church. Ignaz Semmelweis, a nineteenth-century Hungarian doctor, discovered that washing hands could decrease disease, which was contrary to medical belief at the time. Not only did the hospital board not believe him, it refused to reappoint him to the staff, and he died at forty-seven in a state of deep depression. I didn't think I was doing anything that would change the world; I just wanted to try new things that would change my game.

Weren't the teachers being "team players" by following the tradition of not teaching us about black accomplishments? Didn't the mob beating the Freedom Riders see themselves as team players for Southern tradition?

I needed to do some thinking about where team identity ended and individual expression began.

I was struggling with finding my place as a teammate, as a student, as a son, but especially my place in a black world while living in an overwhelmingly white one.

This struggle became particularly important during Easter vacation, when my parents sent me to Goldsboro, North Carolina, to visit family friends. From the Greyhound bus, I witnessed the harsh realities of Southern racism. As soon as the bus crossed the Potomac River into Virginia, store signs like Johnson's White Grocery Store and Corley's White

Luncheonette whizzed by the window. To see racism so boldly out in the open like that shocked me, even though I'd been reading about it for years. Now that I was actually in that world, my stomach clenched in fear. Everyone on the bus was a potential attacker. Would I be hacked to death before the bus even arrived? When I arrived in Raleigh to change buses, I climbed down from the bus as cautiously as an astronaut stepping foot for the first time on Mars. With the brutal slaying of Emmett Till in the back of my mind, I was frightened that I might say or do something that would bring the fiery wrath of white supremacists on me.

Nothing happened. No one attacked me. But, in a way, I attacked myself.

The next day, my head suddenly felt as if hot spikes were being pounded through my skull. I grabbed my head to keep it from exploding. It was another one of my migraines. I staggered into the first dark room I could find, closed the door, and sat there for half an hour in perfect stillness, waiting for the deafening ringing in my ears to go away. Finally, it did and I was able to walk around again, even though I was terrified that it would attack me at any moment.

My worst migraine attacks seemed to come when I was

faced with physical threats. First when I lived under constant abuse at Holy Providence Boarding School, and again when I witnessed open racism in the South. Was my brain acting as some sort of Geiger counter overloading on radioactive racism?

10

Meeting Wilt Chamberlain

The main basketball event before the start of school was the world-famous Rucker Tournament. It was the subject of many articles, books, and documentary movies. It was where wily street hustlers clashed with polished professionals, and the only language spoken fluently was trash talk. I'd gone with my buddy Wesley to see how the game could really be played.

The Rucker Tournament took place at the basketball courts at 128th Street and Seventh Avenue in Harlem. The tournament was started by a local English teacher and playground director, Holcombe Rucker, in 1947 with the emphasis on education. Rucker had been a real hero of Harlem, responsible for more than seven hundred kids getting basketball scholarships to pay for their education. Most experts agree that summer basketball today, from pickup games to organized leagues, owes its existence to Rucker. The Rucker Tournament featured an energetic, flashy style of play, with spinning slam dunks, crossover dribbling, behind-the-back passing, and pretty much anything else that would get the crowd roaring with delight. Basketball historians have credited the Rucker Tournament with forcing the NBA to change its play to the more exciting style fans enjoyed at the tournament. I couldn't play because I was just entering tenth grade, but I would learn more about basketball in one game at Rucker than I would playing an entire season at Power Memorial.

This was basketball as art, with each player eager to display his masterpiece to the crowd. Rather than the predictable, regimented play familiar in team sports, play here was spontaneous, focusing on individual expression coming together in improvised harmony. Each player told his own personal story, but they all discovered how to blend those stories into a common team goal. Among the pros who played here were Julius "Dr. J" Erving, Earl "the Pearl" Monroe, and Wilt "the Stilt" Chamberlain.

And there he was: Wilt Chamberlain! Standing on the sidelines with his own team, he towered over the other players the same way I did.

Wilt was especially famous because a few months earlier he had set a world record by single-handedly scoring 100 points in a 169–147 win by the Philadelphia Warriors over the New York Knicks. No one has ever repeated that extraordinary feat. He set five other league records in that game, including one for free throws. He averaged 50.4 points a game that season, which no one has even come close to matching. There were only two NBA players I could model myself after: Bill Russell (six foot nine) and Wilt (seven foot one). They were big, like me, but they dominated through a balance of power, speed, and agility that made them nearly unstoppable. If I wanted to reach their level of ability, I had to study these men.

Today, Wilt stood at midcourt in his street clothes as if he'd wandered in here by mistake. Then suddenly he was stripping off his street clothes to reveal his tank top and uniform shorts underneath. Like Superman.

I just stood there gaping, unable to take a step or talk.

"Come on, let's just go meet him," Wes said.

"Are you nuts?" I said. "You don't just go up to Wilt Chamberlain and say, 'How's it going, man?'"

"Why not?" he said with a shrug before he started across the blacktop.

Somehow, my feet followed.

Wilt saw us coming. How could he not notice a bony, six-foot-ten, fourteen-year-old kid shuffling toward him in a daze? As we got closer, I realized that even though we shared similar height, he was about twice the size of me in body mass. His arms and legs were thick with muscles. He was twenty-five and in peak physical condition. I felt tiny next to him, and that was not a feeling I was used to.

Wes broke the silence by introducing himself. Then I managed to choke out, "I'm Lew Alcindor."

"Oh yeah, I heard of you," Wilt said with a grin. "You're the young boy that plays for the Catholic school. Supposed to be getting good."

Wilt Chamberlain had heard of me! I couldn't believe it. I rummaged through my mind for something clever to say, but all I could come up with was "I really admire the way you play the game."

As we shook hands, he eyed me up and down. He nodded approvingly. "You've got good legs."

I looked down at my legs and tried to see what he saw. But they just looked like broom-handle legs, nothing special.

"I wish I had legs like that," he said.

What? Wilt Chamberlain wished he had something I had? Impossible!

With nothing left to say and the games about to begin, I said, "Nice to meet you," and hurried away, completely unaware of how much, in just a few years, he would come to influence my life.

11.

The Disappointment
of Winning

At the start of my sophomore year, while I was walking into my barely integrated school, my mind filled with basketball dreams, something amazing happened. The nightly news I watched on TV with my parents was filled with stories about US Air Force veteran James Meredith, the first black student to attend the segregated University of Mississippi. The night before Meredith was scheduled to enroll, more than twenty-five hundred angry white supremacists gathered in a violent protest that left two men dead. The following day, Meredith, accompanied by federal marshals, marched right into that school and enrolled for classes.

To me, James Meredith was like those Western heroes I

loved, defying the shouting lynch mob, walking right past them all as if they didn't exist, head high. *High Noon* in Mississippi. I knew right then that he was the kind of brave and committed man I wanted to become. In the meantime, I had high school.

The team went undefeated my sophomore year. We also took the city championship, which Power Memorial hadn't won since 1939. When that final buzzer echoed through the gym and we were officially the best of the best, I expected to feel something like elation, or completion, or even the satisfaction of rubbing it in the noses of classmates and teachers who thought black people weren't their equals.

Mostly I felt relief that the season was over.

Why didn't I feel better about such a record-breaking season? The team was hugely popular at school. Teachers and students alike treated us with respect and pride. After all, we had elevated the name of the school to national prominence. But with the victories piling up and the whole school swelling with pride, chanting our names at every game, I felt the heavy responsibility of making sure we didn't lose. Winning became less of my focus than not letting down the team, the school, and especially Coach Donahue. Even though Coach drilled into us that it was a team sport, I was sure that if we lost, all the blame would be aimed my way.

Basketball was no longer fun, but more like a tedious job scrubbing toilets that I had no choice but to keep doing. I realized that elation and completion wouldn't be found on the basketball court, no matter how much I won. They would be found by discovering who I was as a black American. And I still hadn't found a coach to teach me that.

Brother Watson was the only black teacher at Power, and I had hoped he would be able to coach me through the internal turmoil I was suffering. He taught French, which seemed a little removed from black culture, but I'd heard he was an amateur drummer, so I thought we might connect through our love of music. One day, I brought in an album by the famous jazz drummer Art Blakey, whose band was called the Jazz Messengers. Art was also known as Abdullah Ibn Buhaina, after becoming a Muslim following his travels to West Africa. That seemed a little weird to me, to change religions like that, especially to one so foreign to American culture. I didn't even know you could change your name, which seemed a pretty rude thing to do to one's parents. I didn't know anything about what Muslims believed, and I didn't really care. The only name I cared about was the nickname he'd gotten from his aggressive drumming style: "Thunder."

I showed Brother Watson the album: *Blue Note 4003*. The whole cover was a photo of Art's serious face sticking up out of a suit, white shirt, and bow tie. He looked as if he were scowling at someone who was trying to pick up his girlfriend. "What do you think of 'Moanin''?" I asked Brother Watson, since that was the album's most famous song.

He took the album in his hands, examined the front and back, and handed it back to me without a glimmer of recognition or even curiosity. "Never heard of him," he said.

"What about Buddy Rich, Elvin Jones, Philly Joe Jones?" I asked.

Blank stare. "Jazz isn't my thing," he said dismissively.

He might as well have poked me in the eye. To me, that was like saying music isn't my thing. Or reading. Or breathing! Listening to jazz was like walking down the street and hearing all the sounds of the city: the traffic, the conversations, the pigeons, the street vendors selling T-shirts or hot dogs. At first, it seems like harsh noise, but when you really focus on how all those sounds come together and harmonize, you realize you're listening to the soundtrack for real life. To me, jazz was a celebration of the spirit. No matter how down and out I felt, jazz could either lift my spirits or take me deeper into my blues until I battled and defeated it.

Herbie Hancock, one of my all-time favorite jazz musicians, offered one of the best descriptions of jazz: "In jazz we share, we listen to each other, we respect each other, we are creating in the moment. At our best, we're non-judgmental." That's how I wanted to see the world, as a team, like my basketball team, in which we all brought our individual strengths and worked together toward some greater good that we couldn't accomplish alone. I also liked the idea that most of the best jazz musicians were black because jazz had its roots in African culture and was developed in America by black musicians in New Orleans. The way that mariachi music came from Mexico and opera originated in Italy.

I didn't know what kind of drumming Brother Watson practiced, but if he didn't know jazz, he clearly wasn't the coach for me in appreciating black culture. I left his classroom that day feeling even more alone. I hadn't been able to connect with the school's one black teacher.

Meanwhile, my religion teacher, Brother D'Adamo, announced in class that "black people want too much too soon." Other students dutifully wrote his words down, but I openly disagreed. What he didn't know was that Brother Harrington, who was in charge of the debate team, had noticed my enthusiasm for talking in class and asked me to join the debate team. Basketball prevented me from joining, but I did accept his invitation to practice oration with the team once a week after school and before basketball. I practiced logic and argumentation with the same intensity that I practiced lay-up drills and wind sprints. I knew how to present an articulate and reasoned opinion, using facts and statistics. That's exactly what I did to Brother D'Adamo and the rest of the class, who clearly agreed with him.

"It seems to me," I explained, "that wanting freedom from oppression a hundred years after the Civil War isn't really 'too soon.' Wanting the same opportunities and justice that whites have, and that are guaranteed to everyone in the Constitution, isn't 'too much.'"

Students shifted uncomfortably in their seats. Challenging a teacher was not usual in a Catholic school.

Brother D'Adamo stiffened. "What I meant was that Negroes must work for their equality."

"How much harder do we have to work than we already are to deserve it?" I said, my heart thumping with a combination of anger and fear. "Why do you, an immigrant from Ireland, deserve it more than blacks who were dragged here two hundred years ago?"

In a movie, the bell would have rung and I would have

marched out triumphantly. But it was real life and Brother D'Adamo simply moved us to another topic, and I sat there feeling both proud and foolish.

That was when I first became He Who Speaks for All Black People. To many white people, we were all one dark entity with a single hive mind. No person can speak for an entire group, but I didn't mind my role because at least I was speaking my own mind. Unfortunately, school tests were based on what the teachers taught us inside the school, and I was determined to keep getting good grades. More often than not, I was forced to regurgitate their words back to them, no matter how wrong I thought they were.

The teachers at Power tried to control my thinking, while Coach Donahue controlled my body. He quarantined me from the press to keep me from getting too full of myself and ruining his endless lessons on teamwork. He was protecting me, but he was also protecting his job. A winning team made him a more valuable commodity for other coaching jobs. But despite his insistence that I not talk to the press, newspapers were writing about me. When the first article appeared, my father showed a rare moment of pride by buying fifteen copies and sending them to relatives.

As our winning season continued, Coach began spending

more time with me. He drove me to school a couple of times a week, and we chatted casually about sports and school. He was cheerful and clearly had my best interests at heart, but there was still something missing. We were friendly without being friends. Still, when we did speak about race issues, he was sympathetic to our plight.

"I saw some bad stuff in the army," he told me. "I was stationed at Fort Knox, Kentucky. Not exactly a state known for racial enlightenment."

I didn't know how to talk about race with an adult, especially a white adult. Especially my coach. I just nodded.

"It's all gonna change someday, Lew," he said as we drove.

"When?" I asked. That was the only thing I cared about.

He sighed. "It'll take generations. Racism won't die out until all the hard-core racists die out. Then each new generation will be a little less racist, until all that hatred is diluted out of existence."

"Generations? That's going to take a long time."

He looked over at me sympathetically. He could see I was not happy with that answer. "All good people can do is wait for justice."

Wait, huh? That way of thinking frustrated me. It was

the same speech I'd been hearing my whole life, from teachers to politicians. Why did we have to be the ones to wait? Racism would die out, I thought, when all reasonable people refused to let it exist. Surely there were enough reasonable white and black people to stomp out racism right now!

That spring, in the middle of our basketball season, Dr. Martin Luther King Jr. was thrown in jail after protesting segregation in Birmingham, Alabama. During his incarceration, he wrote his famous "Letter from Birmingham Jail," in which he encouraged people to disobey immoral laws like segregation. A month later, the television and newspapers were filled with images of a civil rights protest in Birmingham where the authorities attacked protesters with fire hoses and police dogs. Giving the orders was the commissioner of public safety, Eugene "Bull" Connor, who warned that the city "ain't gonna segregate no niggers and whites together." How could we be asked to wait when this was going on? Dr. King expressed my frustration in his letter:

I have almost reached the regrettable conclusion that the Negro's great stumbling block in his stride toward freedom is not

the white Citizen's Counciler or the Ku Klux Klanner, but the white moderate, who is more devoted to "order" than to justice; who prefers a negative peace which is the absence of tension to a positive peace which is the presence of justice; who constantly says: "I agree with you in the goal you seek, but I cannot agree with your methods of direct action"; who paternalistically believes he can set the timetable for another man's freedom; who lives by a mythical concept of time and who constantly advises the Negro to wait for a "more convenient season." Shallow understanding from people of good will is more frustrating than absolute misunderstanding from people of ill will. Lukewarm acceptance is much more bewildering than outright rejection.

In history class, we had studied something similar from the eighteenth-century Irish politician Edmund Burke, who is credited with saying, "The only thing necessary for the triumph of evil is that good men do nothing." And that's what "wait" meant: good people doing nothing. Dr. King had said something about that, too, in his letter: "For years now I have heard the word 'Wait!' It rings in the ear of every Negro with piercing familiarity. This 'Wait' has almost always meant 'Never.' We must come to see, with one of our distinguished jurists, that 'justice too long delayed is justice denied.'"

Unfortunately, waiting is mostly what teenagers do, no matter what race. Adults make it seem like an evil wizard's curse: "Wait until you have children!" "Wait until you're in the real world!" "Wait until you're our age!" What choice did we have but wait while adults ran the world and preached to us how we would one day inherit their mess because we were "the hope of the future." Waiting was our weight.

I was tired of waiting for others to do the right thing. But I was only sixteen. What else could I do?

12

Summer in the City

After school was out for the year, my parents signed me up to attend Coach Donahue's Friendship Farm basketball camp for eight weeks, just as I had the summer before. But this summer I was more excited to hang out with my friends than to play basketball. Life on the streets was varied and surprising. We never knew what was going to happen when we got together. Basketball camp was the same old routines. I knew everything we would do and exactly what Coach would say.

I tried to make the most of the four weeks I had before camp started. I still played basketball, but a whole different kind from what I played on the polished wooden floors of Catholic schools. This was streetball, played on rough asphalt, where every bump and shove could cost you in skin and blood. I traveled all over the city in search of good games, from the Bronx to Long Island to Greenwich Village. Sometimes I would travel an hour or more by subway to get to a choice court.

One of my favorite courts stood on the corner of West Third Street and Sixth Avenue in Greenwich Village and was caged in by a high metal fence. The players were mostly black, with an occasional appearance by an Italian from nearby Little Italy. The games were so intense that spectators often stood three deep against the fence, shouting and jeering during each game. Most of the audience had their favorite players, and sometimes I'd even hear a few chanting, "Lew! Lew! Lew!"

We had no referees, so fouls and other violations were called by the players. Because winners kept the court and losers sat, not all the players were particularly honest in their calls. This led to many heated arguments that sometimes escalated beyond name-calling to physical violence.

Part of the toughness I developed that summer wasn't just from playing streetball or from my newly awakened political awareness, but from the edgy friends I hung out with. Harold was the boldest thief we knew. He didn't break into people's homes or snatch purses off women's shoulders. To him, that didn't show courage or skill. He focused on Woolworth's stores. He would watch the clerks until they walked away from the register. Then he would waltz right up to the cash register, open it, grab all the cash, and run off before anyone saw him.

I didn't approve of what he did, but he was my friend and I didn't think I should judge him. And, I had to admit, there was something thrilling about hanging out with a real thief.

Another friend, Julio, loved basketball as much as I did. We hit plenty of blacktop courts together. Despite Julio's clear intelligence and basketball skills, he'd made up his mind he wanted to be a mobster, as in old movies about Al Capone. He was always looking for an opportunity to cross over into being a full-fledged gangster. One Saturday, after a tough bunch of basketball games at the Greenwich Village court, he grabbed me by the arm and nodded at the man selling ice cream out of his pushcart.

"There's the Good Humor Man," Julio said, nudging me.

"Yeah, so?" I responded.

"So?" He looked at me as if I had spit on his shoes. "So, he must have three, four hundred dollars on him."

At ten cents an ice cream bar, I was suspicious of Julio's math. "So?" I repeated.

Julio sighed. "So, we follow him to where he stores his cart. Then we rob him!"

I looked over at the man handing a chocolate-covered ice cream bar to a woman in a sun hat. He was short and old and overweight. I thought about him going home to his family after a hard day's work in the hot sun with no money to show for it.

I told him I wanted nothing to do with it and took the next train home. Later that summer, while I was away at Friendship Farm, I heard that Julio got arrested. I didn't see him again for ten years.

The rest of the summer was spent swimming and playing basketball with twenty-four other kids at Coach Donahue's Friendship Farm in rural upstate New York. Gone were the vibrant, exciting streets of New York City, where people bustled here and there twenty-four hours a day. Gone were streets altogether. The "farm" part of Friendship Farm wasn't an exaggeration. We slept in a building that had been completed in the 1780s and swam in the Hudson River. At least this year, the court had been paved, and we were no longer playing on just hard dirt. I got along with everyone, so there was no drama, but I didn't have any close friends, either. We were like coworkers at a boring job. Every day was routine, with predictable basketball drills and lackluster games that weren't very challenging or interesting. The difference between the street basketball I'd been playing all over New York City and Friendship Farm basketball was the difference between jazz and elevator music.

The rest of my summer vacation slowly leaked away until I was back in school.

13.

Things Fall Apart

My junior year didn't start with happy thoughts about another championship season, college recruiters, or fans yelling my name.

It started with the murder of black children.

On September 15, 1963, about a week after classes started, whatever hope Dr. King's "I Have a Dream" speech in front of two hundred thousand people at the Lincoln Memorial had given me and other black Americans eighteen days earlier was kicked aside by the bombing of the Sixteenth Street Baptist Church in Birmingham, Alabama, which killed four black girls just as they were preparing for a sermon called "A Love That Forgives."

The damage extended way beyond those crumbled church walls. The shock waves knocked all black Americans to their knees in tears of compassion for the families—and tears of outrage for the America where this kind of morally repugnant act could happen, over and over again.

I felt all the same fury I'd felt over Emmett Till's murder. I was about the same age as three of the girls, and I'd been attending Mass when it happened. Same age, same skin color, in church at the same time. The vulnerability I had experienced previously in North Carolina I now felt all the time. In school. Walking down the street. Buying records in a store. There were white people out there who weren't content to deny us equal rights. They needed to murder us. They murdered children, so no one was safe. They blew up churches, so no place was safe.

I knew we'd be told to wait for justice. I was used to the "Be patient and wait" excuse by now, but it still made me angry. As it turned out, we did have to wait—for fourteen years! In 1965, two years after the bombing, the FBI investigation decided that four Ku Klux Klansmen had committed the murders. However, no one was prosecuted until 1977, fourteen years after the bombing. Even then, only three of the men were charged and convicted, with the fourth alleged conspirator never charged.

Living each day looking over my shoulder, suspicious

that any package could be a bomb, having friends withdraw from my presence, and being unable to have conversations about my feelings and concerns with my parents left me feeling adrift, belonging nowhere with no one.

That year I stayed mostly around Harlem, among other black people. I felt safer there, but I also was becoming more and more interested in politics. I knew there was injustice, but now I was anxious to learn the roots of it and the machinery behind it. The kind of stuff we never even addressed in school.

My attitude carried over into my basketball game. I played much more aggressively, showing everyone that this was one black person who would not be pushed around. I especially liked battling for rebounds, using my body to clear space while snatching the ball off the backboard. Each point I scored was a point for the team, but each ball I grabbed away from the others, pushing and elbowing for it, felt like another point scored for my people. On the court, I wanted to make them feel the way they made me feel off the court: helpless.

We were winning game after game with no losses. We seemed unstoppable. College and university offers came in daily, but I never saw them. Anything with a school letterhead went directly to Coach Donahue without even being opened. My parents had handed the responsibility of my future over to the coach. They didn't feel qualified to figure out which offers were the best, so they relied on the coach to decide my future. That made me a little uncomfortable because as much as I admired the coach and appreciated him, he wasn't family. And even though I had sincere affection for him and I believed he had the same for me, given all that was going on in the world, I wasn't certain I wanted a white man—even a well-meaning one—making choices for me.

I didn't say anything outright, but I did constantly pester him about the letters, which even I hadn't seen.

He tried to calm me. "Lew, don't worry. You can go to any school you want to."

"Did Harvard write me a letter?"

"Don't bother about who's written the letters," he'd assure me. "Any school you want to go to, you can go to."

Despite my small misgivings, I continued to work as hard as I could for him. After all, he held my future in his hands.

All that changed one afternoon. It was a typical winter in New York, cold air whipping around stinging our faces and stiffening our muscles as we marched into the gymnasium. At least the gym floor was toasty as we warmed up against St. Helena's, a Catholic high school in the Bronx. We were feeling pretty cocky since St. Helena's had a weak record and had no reasonable chance against us. We were the league powerhouse, the undisputed, undefeated champions

Even as we warmed up to play, we were really thinking about the game we would playing in two days in Maryland against DeMatha Catholic High School, one of the top high school teams in the country. They would be a real challenge, and if we hoped to beat them, we would have to muster all our skills and determination. But first we had to dispose of pesky St. Helena's, a minor detour on our way to glory. I figured we would be up at least twenty points by halftime and then coast to an easy victory in the last half. At least we would put on a good show for the home crowd, which had been filling up all the seats at our games.

When the halftime buzzer sounded, we were up only six points, which in basketball is meaningless. A team can turn that around in a minute or two. Our whole team was in shock. We had been smug and arrogant, and it showed in our lackluster performance. I was playing especially poorly and couldn't seem to get back on track. Most athletes know to never approach any competition underestimating your opponent because it lowers your level of play, even if you don't mean for that to happen. And once that does happen, it's very difficult to climb back up to the level you're used to.

As the team filed out of the gym for halftime break, I could hear how much quieter the crowd was than usual. Murmurs instead of laughter. They were probably in disbelief at our poor performance, and a little worried that we were about to break our undefeated streak. I was, too. Our heads hung low, we quietly trooped down the cold stairwell to the locker room and crowded into Coach Donahue's office. His office was already small, made smaller by the desk and filing cabinets. The single window was fogged over from the cold outside and the heat steaming off our bodies. We plopped down on the old wooden chairs, the sweat from our arms and legs dripping onto the floor.

Coach closed the door and snapped the lock into place. When he turned to look at us, his face was contorted with anger. We were used to his angry tirades at practice, but this was a whole new level of wrath. He began ranting and raving, marching around the cramped office as if standing still would cause him to spontaneously burst into flames.

"You don't deserve to win!" he raged. "You're terrible! A mess!"

We didn't dare say anything. Besides, we didn't really disagree.

"You're a disgrace, playing like you're sleepwalking!"

Again, he wasn't wrong. We didn't dare look at him because we knew we deserved every word.

And then he turned his anger on me. His face red with fury, he pointed at me. "And you, Lew! You go out there and don't hustle. You don't move. You don't do any of the things you're supposed to do." He glared with burning eyes. "You're acting just like a *nigger!*"

A sharp pain pierced my heart as if he'd just stabbed me with a butcher knife. My throat tightened as if he were choking me with his other hand. The skin on my arms and legs was ice-cold, but my face burned with unbearable heat. I looked him straight in his angry face, but I was too shocked to say anything. An image came to me of my ex–best friend Johnny yelling "Nigger!" in my face.

Since Johnny, I'd been especially protective so that something like this couldn't happen again. I'd been careful not to hang around with people who I thought were racist in any way, even if they didn't know it themselves. Most of the racists I'd met in school didn't think they were racists. They thought their negative comments about black people or

Puerto Ricans or Jews were just facts. To them, black people *were* lazy, Puerto Ricans *were* criminals, Jews *were* cheats. That's what they'd been told all their lives, so it must be true. I made sure I stayed away from those people and surrounded myself with people I could trust.

People like Coach Donahue.

With the word "nigger" still echoing in my brain, I just sat there forcing myself to breathe.

I played the second half in a daze, like someone just told he had six weeks to live. I don't remember anything about the game, the plays we made or didn't make, the reaction of the crowd, words spoken to me by my teammates.

We won.

On the way to the locker room, I was told I played well. I just nodded.

I stood under the hot shower trying to collect my thoughts. My world had changed so drastically, it was like everything was on a tilt and I couldn't get my footing. The adult I trusted most, besides my parents, I could no longer trust.

Coach Donahue had been a protective wall against the outside world. Now that wall was gone. Worse, he was part of the outside world I needed protection from.

After my shower, I dressed mechanically, trying to decide what I would tell my parents. They had placed my future in this man's hands.

"Lew," Coach Donahue said, standing at the end of the row of lockers. "My office." He gestured for me to follow him.

Like a zombie, I rose and followed him into his office. The pain I felt just being in his presence was unbearable.

"See!" he said with a huge smile. "It worked! My strategy worked. I knew that if I used that word, it'd shock you into a good second half. And it did!" He sat on the edge of the desk and beamed at me happily.

I didn't say anything.

"I know it seemed harsh at the time, but it got you going."

I still said nothing.

He kept talking excitedly about the lesson to be learned from this, about how it was his job to use any means necessary to make sure I played up to my potential, about strategies to play DeMatha. He could have been talking about space travel for all the attention I paid him. I understood what was going on. He was trying to justify using that word as a motivator and thought I should be grateful because we won. He had no idea that he'd crossed a line that there was no coming back from.

In his mind, by telling me not to play like a nigger, he was telling me that I was acting like the stereotype that many white people had of a black person: lazy, slow, unfocused. He didn't want the crowd or the other team or even my own teammates to think of me that way, so I needed to apply myself more. But that meant he saw most black people as that stereotype. He believed most black people didn't apply themselves, ignoring the fact that politicians kept them from having the same educational and job opportunities as white people.

I left his office feeling more alone than I'd felt since boarding school.

We were supposed to leave for the Maryland game right away, so I went home to pack. All the way home, I wondered how I'd be able to play with the team again, and whether I'd be able even to look at Coach without my anger and sadness getting the better of me.

When I got home, I told my parents what had happened. They both were outraged, feeling just as angry and betrayed as I did.

"I'm done," I told them. "I can't go back to Power."

I wanted to transfer immediately to one of the other local high schools. Doing so meant I would lose a year of eligibility and have to do an extra year of high school, but I didn't care. I couldn't spend one more minute around Coach Donahue. How could I play to win when winning would confirm what he'd done as being right?

My parents were sympathetic to my feelings, but they didn't want anything to get in the way of my going to college as soon as possible. For that to happen, I would have to finish the season, playing for Coach Donahue. Despite their anger, they wanted to do what was best for my future. But all I could see was my own rage. Couldn't they understand that even being in the same room with that man was asking too much? In the end, however, I didn't have a choice. I needed my parents' permission to transfer, and I wasn't going to get it.

The train ride to Maryland was subdued. The team had heard what Coach Donahue had said, and they didn't know how to react. We used to joke at the names he'd called us, but now no one was in a joking mood. If Coach sensed the change in his team or in me, he never spoke about it. He continued as if nothing had happened. Maybe in his mind, nothing had.

We played DeMatha Catholic High School, the team we'd worried so much about, and beat them. I played hard, not so much to please Coach Donahue, but to show the rest of the team that I wasn't affected by what he said. I couldn't show any weakness, or someone else might call me that name.

We finished the season undefeated, then won the city championship for the second year in a row. We were chosen as the number one Catholic high school team in the country, and I was once again selected for the All-City and All-American teams. It should have been a season of triumph and happiness, but it wasn't. It ended in bitterness and anger.

14

Final Confrontation
with Coach Donahue

When my junior year ended, I figured I was rid of Coach Donahue, at least for the three months of summer. I certainly wouldn't be attending his Friendship Farm basketball camp again. But I didn't want to roam the streets playing basketball, staring shyly at girls I didn't have the nerve to talk to, and doing nothing significant. There was too much going on in the outside world for me to sit by idly. I was determined to participate. Somehow.

I applied to the Heritage Teaching Program for the Harlem Youth Action Project (HARYOU-ACT), a city-sponsored antipoverty program designed to keep kids off the streets and teach us about our African American heritage. I was accepted into its journalism workshop as a reporter at a salary of $35 a week, which is equal to about $272 today. I wanted to prove that I was worth every penny.

Everything about the job excited me. I was thrilled to be working in Harlem, which was the cultural center of African Americans in New York City. Although I'd been born there, we'd moved away when I was too young to get to know the place or the people. Sure, I occasionally went to Harlem to grab a bite to eat or play a few games of streetball with the locals, but then I immediately hopped the subway and returned home again. I had always loved being in Harlem, and now I could explore it to my heart's content.

And I couldn't wait to learn more about my African American heritage. In 1964, very little was written, broadcast, or openly discussed about black history or culture. Hardly any black characters appeared in movies or on TV, and the few who did were generally background figures who silently served meals or chauffeured for rich white people. For comic relief, they'd occasionally throw in a boisterous black character who dressed outrageously and spoke loudly and with poor grammar. My teachers at school were no help in dispelling these stereotypes. Either they were ignorant of black history or they didn't think it worth teaching—I couldn't decide which was worse.

Equally important, I would be writing. My English teachers had always praised my writing ability, even reading some of my papers aloud in class. But this wasn't class. I would be writing articles that people would read outside the safety of the classroom. This would be a whole new challenge, and as much as the competitor in me was excited by the challenge, I was also scared. With basketball, everything was immediate: You shot the ball and either you scored or you didn't, you won the game or you didn't, but you judged your success or failure right away. With writing, you composed your ideas, wrote and rewrote them until you couldn't stand to read them again, printed them, sent them out to readers, and waited for their response. The wait would be nerve-racking.

At least the summer was mine to succeed or fail in. No more Coach Donahue to please.

Or so I thought.

When Coach Donahue discovered I wasn't returning to Friendship Farm, he was truly surprised.

"Lew, what do you mean you're not coming back?" he asked.

"I've made other plans," I said, unwilling to confront him.

I could see he was totally clueless how much he'd hurt me. "But I refurbished the whole camp and placed advertisements. For the first time, we have paying campers who aren't just from Power." Thanks to me and the rest of the team, his reputation as a coach had grown, and he was ready to reap the rewards. "You've got to come, Lew," he pleaded. "You're a draw to the new campers."

I really wanted to tell him what I thought of him and his camp. I wanted to write those words ten feet high on the sides of buildings and on subway cars, to carry my message throughout the city so everyone knew just how I felt. I now was in the position to hurt Coach Donahue the same way he had hurt me—through betrayal. He had betrayed my trust in him to protect me, and I could betray his trust in me to support his camp. I could have my revenge on him. All I had to do was not go.

The thing was, though, the Good Boy in me still felt as if I owed him. He had taken me to see pro ball games, he had driven me to school, he had coached me from a skinny, awkward kid to a powerhouse player with scholarship offers from across the country. Basically, he was a good man and a good teacher. But the fact that he didn't seem to know what he had done that was so bad showed how he saw me only as a basketball player helping him win games, not as an individual, seventeen-year-old black kid, who had to face a hostile environment every day. Still, I felt as if it would be wrong of me to punish him for being who he was rather than who I wanted him to be.

I agreed to attend Friendship Farm for three weeks in August. He was happy, my mother was happy, and I was, if not happy, satisfied that I'd paid him back in full. After this, I owed him nothing. I would be free.

15

Meeting Dr. Martin Luther King Jr.

My HARYOU journalism workshop was located in the Harlem Branch YMCA, on West 135th Street. The main building, constructed in 1931–32, looked like twin brick towers with a shorter connecting brick building, resembling a Lego version of a medieval castle. Part of my ignorance of my own culture then was that I didn't know the significance of what I thought was just another YMCA, like the hundreds across the country. I didn't know that it was built especially for African American men because most of the other YMCAs were only for white men. I didn't know that the famed civil rights leader Malcolm X had stayed there as a young man. I didn't know that the celebrated Jamaican American writer Claude McKay had lived there for five years. I didn't know that the scientist George Washington Carver, baseball superstar Jackie Robinson, and singer-actor Paul Robeson had either stayed or performed there.

My own cultural heritage had been around me all this time, but I hadn't really noticed it. Now I looked for it everywhere and was constantly rewarded.

The inside of the YMCA had various murals by famous black artists such as William E. Scott and Aaron Douglas, whose work appears in the National Gallery of Art and the Metropolitan Museum of Art. Douglas's mural *Evolution of Negro Dance* filled one archway with its dark silhouettes of black people going through stages of social development from crouching in enslavement in dark shadows to celebrating freedom by dancing in the light. Looking at that beautiful mural, I instantly felt connected to the evolution portrayed. Like them, I had started in the dark about who I was, being the person everyone expected me to be without really knowing who *I* wanted to be. Then, through the physical rigors of basketball and the mental discipline of reading, I had stood tall and stepped out of the shadows into the bright sunlight of finding myself.

Unfortunately, that bright sunlight was mostly symbolic

because our actual office was located way down in the gloomy, windowless basement of the building. Our "sunlight" was provided by buzzing fluorescent lights; our "dancing" was rushing back and forth on squeaky linoleum floors, yellow and brittle with age. Despite the relentless summer heat on the streets above, we were always in a humid coolness that felt like a damp cave. I would not have been surprised to arrive one morning and find bats hanging from the ceiling.

The room itself was about forty feet square, equipped with ancient black metal typewriters that required a lot of pressure to force the keys to impact the paper. These typewriters were always in use, so the room continually echoed with a loud clickety-clack. We often had to raise our voices to hear one another. The room also housed a typesetting machine that seemed so old that Benjamin Franklin might have used it to print *Poor Richard's Almanack*.

But we were all filled with youthful passion and energy, ready to bring our fresh ideas and enthusiasm to the Harlem community.

The man in charge of our young group of fired-up journalists was Al Calloway. However, the head of the Heritage Teaching Program was Dr. John Henrik Clarke. He was about fifty years old and had kind eyes that never stopped analyzing, yet never seemed to be judging. His smile was warm and he spoke softly, but with the precision and forcefulness of an academic, which he was. Dr. Clarke was a well-known historian who had published various notable articles, had cofounded the *Harlem Quarterly*, had been an editor of the *Negro History Bulletin*, had taught at the New School for Social Research, and was a prominent leader in the black political community. He had been born to sharecroppers in Alabama and traveled alone by freight train to Harlem when he was only eighteen. After putting himself through school, he changed his name from John Henry Clark to John Henrik (after the famous Norwegian playwright Henrik Ibsen) Clarke (adding an "e"). It was weird how many people I was running across who had changed their names: the jazz drummer Art Blakey to Abdullah Ibn Buhaina; Malcolm Little to Malcolm X; a few months earlier, in March, the world heavyweight boxing champion Cassius Clay had changed his name to Muhammad Ali. Now Dr. Clarke. It seemed as if people were all reinventing themselves to be who they wanted rather than what others said they had to be.

I couldn't believe how lucky I was to be spending my

summer with a man like Dr. Clarke. I had always loved history, and here I was in the presence of a black man who was also a writer, a historian, a teacher, and an activist. He showed me I didn't have to be defined by just doing one thing. I also realized that he and I had gone through similar awakening experiences in terms of what we had been taught—or rather, *not* taught—about African American history. When Dr. Clarke had been a young Sunday school teacher, he had been disturbed about never seeing any images of dark-skinned people in the Bible. "I began to suspect that something had gone wrong in history," he once said. "I see Moses going down to Ethiopia, where he marries Zipporah, Moses' wife, and she turns white. I see people going to the land of Kush, which is the present day Sudan, and they got white. I see people going to Punt, which is present day Somalia, and they got white. What are all these white people doing in Afrika? There were no Afrikans in Afrika in the Sunday School lesson."

I had wondered the same thing, but my cover of keeping a low profile meant I kept my questions to myself.

But Dr. Clarke didn't stop digging. He read a copy of *The New Negro*, an anthology of essays, fiction, art, and poetry compiled by Alain Locke. The book was famous for helping to define the goals of the Harlem Renaissance, a literary, artistic, musical, and political movement in the 1920s and 1930s that made Harlem one of the most influential centers of cultural influence in America. The awakening that was churning in Harlem sent ripples throughout the country that had an effect on American culture ever since.

Dr. Clarke shared his passion for African American history with all of us, but I felt as if his message were directly aimed at me.

Everything started to make sense to me. Coach Donahue had taught me how to play basketball, how to win games, but Dr. Clarke was teaching me how to find my place within my own community, within my own history. In a way, it was appropriate that my cultural awakening came as a result of being called the N-word. I had been a little too comfortable being the young basketball star, a little out of reach of the kind of dangerous racism that others faced on a daily basis. Ironically, it was Coach Donahue who, by immersing me in basketball, kept me insulated from that real world—and it was Coach Donahue who reminded me that such insulation was a fantasy that could be shattered whenever he wanted to.

That was all over now. Dr. Clarke encouraged us to explore our own past as well as what was going on in the streets around us. Coach Donahue wanted us to become great basketball players, to achieve personal success; Dr. Clarke wanted us to become great African Americans, to enlighten ourselves and others. He hoped that by training Harlem's youth in areas such as art, music, social work, photography, and journalism, those trainees would be able to make Harlem a better place when they became adults.

Al Calloway was our boss. He taught us journalism. Our job as journalists was to produce a weekly paper for the Harlem community that featured the accomplishments of the other HARYOU workshops, in dance, music, and community action, and reported on Harlem life in general. We arrived at ten o'clock in the morning eager for our assignments, then scattered to do research. Some of that was done on the streets by interviewing people, but a lot took place at what is now called the Schomburg Center for Research in Black Culture. Once merely a collection at a branch of the city library, the Schomburg became one of the world's richest sources for learning about black history, thanks to the Puerto Rican–born black scholar Arturo Alfonso Schomburg, who donated his enormous collection of books on black history.

Walking into that building for the first time was like walking across the burning desert and being handed a glass of ice water. I hadn't even known how thirsty I was until I saw all the books on black history.

The Schomburg became a peaceful place that inspired self-examination. I returned again and again to wander up and down the stacks, pulling every book of interest and plopping myself down at a table to read everything I could. I pored over every sacred scrap of information I could find about the legends of the Harlem Renaissance: the black nationalist Marcus Garvey, black revolutionary W. E. B. Du Bois, poets Langston Hughes and Countee Cullen, fiction writers Zora Neale Hurston and Wallace Thurman. All these talented and earnest young men and women were posing all the same questions that had been bothering me all my life, but I'd never found anyone I could ask. Now I didn't have to. I could just read their insightful words and feel myself filling up, not just with knowledge but also with pride. How could I be a senior in high school and not even have heard of the Harlem Renaissance?

Now I studied everything I could about it. At the Schomburg, I was learning about the past just as history was in the process of happening right in front of me. It was clear that Big Changes were happening all around me. The more I read about the past, the more I understood about the present conflicts. Now I just had to figure out what I wanted from the future.

After a long session at the Schomburg, I would walk out onto the streets and notice some of the similarities between the Harlem of the Renaissance era and the Harlem now. Unrest, frustration, and distrust were as thick as the humid summer air. Black militants such as Malcolm X preached about injustice from the same soapboxes that Marcus Garvey had used. Malcolm X's Nation of Islam, which advocated an aggressive "by any means necessary" approach to achieving racial equality, was at odds with the strict nonviolence advocated by Dr. Martin Luther King Jr. At one speech in Harlem that month, some Black Muslims from the Nation of Islam actually threw stones at Dr. King because they felt his message of nonviolence was holding back black equality. Racial tensions had gone far beyond just black versus white; now they were also black versus black.

I was still trying to decide where I stood. Dr. King had been chosen as *Time* magazine's Man of the Year at the beginning of 1964 and was a beloved leader of many black people. He was a kind, gentle man but a forceful and passionate speaker. He was convinced that the nonviolence preached by Jesus and practiced by Gandhi would be effective in the civil rights movement. While I admired his courage, dedication, ability to inspire, and even his optimism, I wasn't convinced that nonviolence was realistic. Especially after the news in June that James Chaney, a black activist from Mississippi, and Andrew Goodman and Michael Schwerner, white New Yorkers seeking to help register black voters in the area as part of the Freedom Summer project, had gone missing. After a desperate search by hundreds of volunteers, their bodies were discovered about six weeks later. Eventually, some twenty men, including police officers who had handed the civil rights workers over to their murderers in the middle of the night, would be indicted. How could nonviolently marching and singing "We Shall Overcome" combat this kind of violence? I had no answers, but I knew that when Dr. King spoke, all things did indeed seem possible, even "a community where men can live together without fear."

Despite my newfound intellectual curiosity, I still had to maintain my physical fitness for basketball. Since we were already headquartered in a YMCA, I took advantage of the gym facilities. When I walked into the workout room, I was surprised to see jazz great Miles Davis punching the speed bag and Wilt Chamberlain hefting weights.

Wilt recognized me from our previous meeting. At six foot eleven, I was hard to forget.

"Still makin' a name for yourself, huh, kid?" he said as he curled dumbbells larger than my head.

"Trying," I said.

"You're going to need to pack on some meat if you want to bang with the big boys." He grinned and plopped the dumbbells onto the ground with a loud clank. Then he picked up a barbell with even bigger weights. "You need muscle if you're going to jump up with three guys climbing on your back."

I looked at his thick muscles with envy. I felt like a pencil standing next to a mailbox.

"I'll work on it," I promised, then grabbed a barbell that was too heavy for me, struggling to raise it. If he noticed, he didn't let on, which I appreciated more than the advice.

After that encounter, our run-ins at the gym weren't always accidental. I knew when Wilt was around because I only had to look across the street from the YMCA to see his black limo or fuchsia Bentley parked outside. I started shooting baskets at break time whenever he was there, and one time he actually came and started shooting around with me.

"Wanna try a little one-on-one?" he asked with a grin.

"Nope." I wasn't even tempted. If he ran into me, I'd be nothing but a long stain on the floor. "How about H-O-R-S-E?"

"H-O-R-S-E it is," he said and spun around to sink a ten-foot fadeaway.

I matched his shot.

He laughed. "This is going to be fun."

It was fun. We tossed in hooks, reverse lay-ups, long bombs—anything we could think of. He won the game, but I won, too, because now we had a speaking relationship.

When I wasn't plotting to accidentally run into Wilt, I focused on my job as a journalist. Much of what we wrote was fairly routine promotion for local history and events. But one day, we received unexpected good news. That June, Dr. Martin Luther King Jr., as a favor to Dr. Clarke, agreed to address participants in the HARYOU program. And I was chosen to attend the press conference after his talk.

I showed my press credentials to gain admittance to the conference. They made me feel so adult and powerful, like guys on TV who flipped open a wallet to flash an FBI badge. Once in the room, I saw Dr. King sitting at the small table in front of a half-dozen microphones, two men on either side of him. He looked calm and happy, with a round face like a black cherub. He looked like a man you could confide anything to and he would smile, pat you on the back, and say, "How can I help?"

I felt a little light-headed, realizing suddenly that I was not just observing history but actually participating. I stood among the crowd of seasoned reporters, a tall, skinny, seventeen-year-old kid holding a battered tape recorder to capture Dr. King's every word. I towered about a foot over the other reporters, yet they were doing all the talking while I just stood there, my hands shaking as I tried to work up the courage to ask a question. I had played basketball in front of crowds of hundreds of people without a second thought, but just standing here in the presence of such a man of vision and purpose made me as nervous as a child about to receive a booster shot. I didn't want this once-in-a-lifetime chance to pass me by, but there were so many serious professionals in their dark suits and ties, and I was just a shy kid in casual street clothes working out of a basement in Harlem.

I don't know where the courage came from, but I finally croaked out a question of my own: "Dr. King, what do you think the significance of Dr. Clarke's program is to the people of Harlem?" Dr. King leaned toward the microphone and said, "I have no doubt that the program will be a great success." He said more about the importance of such programs in guiding the youth of Harlem, but it was hard to hear his words over the thundering thumping of my heart against my ribs.

When I left the conference, I knew that Dr. King was right about the program being a success because it had already transformed me. I felt like a serious person with serious goals. I now understood what I wanted to do with my life. Maybe not the exact details, but I knew that like Dr. King, I had to do something that affected the African American community in a positive way.

16.

Harlem Explodes!

During my many hours at the Schomburg, I discovered the poetry of Langston Hughes, an especially influential writer during the Harlem Renaissance. One poem in particular, called "Harlem," affected me greatly because it asks the same question many African Americans were asking: If the people in power continued to deny black people their shot at the American Dream, would the frustration lead to violence? The poem captured everything I'd been thinking about for a long time. The fact that it was written in 1951 and that we were still asking the same questions in 1964 explained the frustration fueling black leaders like Malcolm X, who urged us to take more aggressive and confrontational actions to obtain our dream of equal rights and opportunities. Black communities were tired of waiting, tired of the same old political promises that those rights and opportunities would eventually come if they would just be "good Negroes" and be patient. Many were tired of being patient, watching white children thrive while their children didn't.

On July 18, 1964, that festering frustration exploded on the streets of Harlem.

It was a hot, muggy Saturday. The dense humidity soaked people's clothes with sweat and irritability. Everything felt heavier, thicker. Every small task seemed to take longer, like we were wading through a swamp. I was returning home from a lazy day reading at the beach, hoping this would be my last summer in New York City before going off to college. I decided to get off the train at 125th Street to stop in a jazz record store and check out the new releases. Since I was already in the area, I thought I'd also use the opportunity to walk over to the CORE (Congress of Racial Equality) rally a few blocks away to see if there was anything newsworthy I could write about for our journal. The rally was taking place to protest the shooting death of a fifteen-year-old African American, James Powell, by a white off-duty police officer, Lieutenant Thomas Gilligan. The shooting had occurred two days before, and there'd been protests throughout the city since.

When I climbed the stairs from the subway to the street, I felt as if I were stepping into a war movie.

Except this wasn't a movie. Real gunshots cracked the air. Real glass windows shattered. Real people screamed in terror as they ran past me looking for cover.

I ducked behind a lamppost, looking around to see where the shots were coming from so I could run in the opposite direction. I saw a couple of men across the street throw a chunk of concrete through a storefront window. Every loud sound spurred the people to run even faster.

I found out later that the riot had started outside the 123rd Street police station, a couple of blocks from where I was huddling in fear. A thousand people had gathered to protest the death of James Powell. Then rocks, bricks, and bottles had been hurled, garbage cans set on fire, and retail stores looted, including those selling guns. A police officer with a megaphone had tried to calm the situation by shouting, "Go home! Go home!" Someone in the crowd had shouted back, "We *are* home, baby!"

I ran. I ran as hard and as fast as I could, afraid my height would make me an easy target for a nervous cop and I'd end up like the fifteen-year-old kid whose death had started this riot. I crouched as I ran, making myself as small as possible—which wasn't small enough: I still loomed over the rest of the people. I had never been so scared in my life, or so sure a stray bullet might punch through my back at any second.

Even as I ran, adrenaline pumping my heart like a boxer's speed bag, I also felt a shared rage with the people running beside me. As much as I admired Dr. King, I, too, wanted to pick up a brick and throw it. Not just for James Powell but also for Emmett Till. And because of Coach Donahue. And the teachers at Power who didn't think it was important to teach us about anyone with a black face.

I didn't throw anything. My readings at the Schomburg had taught me that looting and bricks didn't create any real change. Some government suits would make a sympathetic speech, create a panel that would investigate the causes, dump some money on a couple of neighborhoods, plant a few trees here and there, and hope the dragon would go back to sleep for another ten years. Then it would be some other politician's problem.

The next morning at the journal office, we couldn't stop talking about what had happened.

"That was some bad mojo, man," Sammy said, sitting on the edge of his desk. He wore a white, short-sleeved shirt and narrow blue tie to look more like a professional reporter. The rest of us dressed as casually as we could get away with to combat the thick summer heat.

"It's happening all over the country," Gary said. He stroked his upper lip every ten seconds to check on the barely visible mustache he was trying to grow. "Black folk aren't going to put up with this crap anymore."

"You think it's over?" Sandy asked. Her family was black Portuguese.

"Yeah," Sammy said. "The cops will be waiting for them if they try anything. And they won't be playing around."

"I don't think it's over," Gary said. "Last night is just the beginning. Too much anger to get out in one night."

He looked at me. I was the only one who hadn't said anything. The others looked at me, too. Waiting.

"I was there," I said quietly.

"Really?" Sandy asked with wide eyes.

I nodded. "Gunshots were popping all around me. People running every which way. Guys were smashing windows and grabbing TVs."

"Were you scared?" Sammy asked.

I hesitated. I didn't want to admit in front of them, especially Sandy, just how scared I'd been. I thought about putting on my game face, the stony expression I used when I took the gym floor. But we were journalists, devoted to uncovering the truth.

"I was terrified," I admitted. "I ran like a dog with his tail on fire."

"Can I quote you?" Sammy asked. "Big-time basketball star Lew Alcindor said, 'I nearly peed my pants.'" He grinned. "I'm paraphrasing."

We all laughed. Then we got down to the business of reporting what had happened. Newspapers and television news were filled with images. Many of the headlines focused on the numbers: how many rioters, how many police, how much property damage. But we decided to try to get the more human side of the story. We would go out and interview people on the streets and get their perspectives about what had happened and what it meant to them. The people we interviewed did not hesitate to tell us what they thought: They were angry about the looting and the property damage, but mostly they were angry that another black child had been shot by a police officer, knowing he would probably go free. (He did.)

That night the rioting resumed, this time spreading all the way to the Bedford-Stuyvesant section of Brooklyn. The city authorities declared a state of emergency in Harlem and banned all demonstrations. A "state of emergency"? Were they kidding? Harlem had been in a state of emergency for thirty years; that's why people were rioting! And that's exactly what we wrote about. Meanwhile, the white press was busy condemning Harlemites as a bunch of thugs looking for an excuse to loot a new TV. Yeah, there was some of that. But that was like saying the Boston Tea Party was a bunch of looters after free tea. Did we really fight in the American Revolution so we could get cheaper tea?

In the end, everything gets reduced to numbers. The riots went on for six days, 4,000 New Yorkers were involved in the protests, 118 were injured, 465 were arrested, and one rioter was killed. An FBI report would describe the riots as an attack on "all constituted authority." Our little band of teenage reporters told them that much in our journal. More important, we told them why. As usual, no one was listening.

Our summer program ended that week, and the following week I was back at Coach Donahue's Friendship Farm. After everything I had just been through—being exposed to the Schomburg collection, discovering the rich cultural history of the Harlem Renaissance, meeting Dr. King, being caught in the middle of a riot, writing about the anger and frustrations of people in Harlem—even looking at the name Friendship Farm made me want to break something. But for the sake of my parents and whatever I owed Coach Donahue, I endured my three-week sentence in silence.

At camp, I was a celebrity, with kids fawning over me, joking with me, trying hard to be my friend. They did nothing wrong, but after my experiences in Harlem, I was still in too much of a state of shock to be very friendly. To be honest, I didn't try very hard. To me, being friendly would be an endorsement of Coach Donahue, and I didn't want to send that message. Not after everything I'd been through. People like Coach Donahue, who wanted us to wait our turn, who felt entitled to use the N-word whenever it suited them, were part of the reason for the riots. And they would never admit or understand why they were.

So I acted my part. I played basketball, kept to myself, and, three weeks later, returned to Harlem. As I walked along the streets, I realized that this summer had been a rite of passage for me, a leap from being a child of the projects to being a citizen of Harlem. I had met new coaches, like Al Calloway, Dr. Clarke, and Dr. King, who had held up a mirror so I could see myself clearly for the first time. Now I knew what my history was, who my people were, and where my future pointed.

17

Making Friends with Wilt Chamberlain

The last couple of weeks until the start of my senior year, I tried to get back to a normal life of hanging with friends and playing intense streetball. I returned to Harlem frequently, now that I felt so much at home there. Harlem was busily repairing the physical damage caused by the riots, but everything was not business as usual. White politicians and news commentators expected Harlemites to be repentant and act ashamed, like naughty children who had broken their parents' favorite vase. Instead, they walked around a little taller, with a little more pride. They had a "you know why" look in their eyes and an expectant "what are you going to do to fix it" expression on their faces. Most residents had not wanted the burning, the destruction, the looting, but sometimes those were the unfortunate by-products of legitimate peaceful protests. And doing nothing would have been worse. How many unarmed black children could they allow to be killed without saying something?

I missed my involvement with HARYOU and the opportunity to put into words all the thoughts and emotions I had experienced during the turmoil. I discovered I had a passion for writing that ran much deeper than I'd realized. Not just a passion but a need to somehow get it all out of me. Without that creative outlet, I had to express myself on the basketball court. I played every chance I could, any place I could find a game. Then, when the summer Rucker Tournament started, I made sure I was there to watch the best players in the world teach me how to become better.

Wilt was there with his own team from Big Wilt's Smalls Paradise, the Harlem nightclub he owned. I gave him a wave, he nodded back, and I settled in to watch him play. The battle against Wilt's team looked to be pretty even at first, but then the other team started to pull ahead. Wilt was fuming. For three quarters, Wilt endured the pounding, until he decided he just wouldn't take any more.

I could see the determination not just in his face, but in

his whole body. Wilt refused to lose. He went after every rebound and grabbed it no matter how many other players also went after it. His teammates fed him the ball under the basket and he dunked it. If Wilt got his hands on the ball, he dunked it. And there was nothing they could do to stop him. He dunked ten times in a row, with the crowd screaming in delight at the show he was putting on. Sometimes he'd go up with three players hanging on to him. But they might as well have been fluffy scarves for all the trouble they caused. Watching him, I learned the advantage of sheer willpower in winning a game. It was a lesson that stayed with me my entire basketball career.

"That was amazing," I said to him afterward.

"We got it done," he said. No boasting. No grinning.

I mangled a few more appreciative compliments while he toweled the sweat from his face and neck.

"Tell you what, young Lewis," he said. "Why don't you drop by Smalls sometime. We'll talk."

Then he was gone, he and his team shaking hands in the crowd.

I did drop by Smalls a couple of days later, not wanting to seem too eager. It wasn't just that Wilt Chamberlain was one of the best players in the world, or that there was a cool, edgy allure to being seventeen and hanging out in a night-club. The real appeal for me was that Wilt was the living embodiment of my possible future. Whatever he was doing right now was probably what I could be doing in five years. I needed to learn what that life would be like.

I learned that his life was good. I'd had a small taste of celebrity from the press swarming me during my All-City games, but nothing like the relentless recognition that Wilt got. No matter where he went, fans would yell and wave and run up to him as if he were their old high school pal. Inside Smalls, he could control that public adulation somewhat by carving out a space and surrounding himself with close friends. Wilt's entourage at Smalls warmly welcomed me to the group, even going so far as concocting a special non-alcoholic drink just for me. They called it the Orange Sling, which consisted of orange juice with an egg beaten into it. I couldn't believe I was sitting in one of the hippest joints in Harlem, sipping a signature drink with Wilt Chamberlain. Life had certainly taken a turn for the better.

One day, we were in Smalls when Wilt decided we should go to his apartment to play cards. We all piled into his limo and drove to his home in the ritzy Park West Village complex on Central Park West.

Wilt's apartment was the ultimate bachelor pad, with antique gold finish on everything in sight. The walls were decorated with real paintings, not just cheap copies from Woolworth's as most people I knew had. His stereo system was the latest in high-tech, surrounded by a large record collection with some of the same jazz albums I owned. Only more. Much, much more. Wilt had a reputation for extravagance, but this was all beyond even my imagination. This was where Frank Sinatra or Dean Martin might live in one of their rollicking movies about chasing girls.

For the first time, I had a coach who was teaching me the possibilities of a successful black man's lifestyle. If this was the lifestyle I had in store for me, then bring it on!

Wilt made a point of taking me to swanky places, giving me a taste of what my life would be like one day. Having been brought up in a working-class family and neighborhood, my imagination for spending was limited to slick photographs in upscale magazines. I couldn't really think of what I would do with money beyond a fancy suit and hot car. One evening, he took Carl Green, me, and my date, Sandy from HARYOU—whom I finally got up the nerve to ask out—to the Latin Quarter, a popular and swanky nightclub. Sandy wore her hair like Diana Ross, up in the back with straight bangs over her forehead, and a simple summer dress with straps. I wore my best—and only—suit, with a skinny black tie. We looked just like what we were: a couple of high schoolers playing dress-up. Carl and Wilt wore tailored suits and shiny ties that made them look as if they owned the place. And that's how they were treated. The waitstaff hovered around us like fawning grandparents, making sure we had everything we wanted. The singer from the stage announced, "We have a celebrity in the audience," and a bright spotlight swept over the room until it lit up our table. I shrank back into my seat, looking for a shadow to hide in. Wilt seemed to puff up under the light, like a sponge expanding in water. The diners cheered and Wilt waved back, the wattage from his smile rivaling that of the spotlight.

For the rest of that summer, Wilt was my guru into this fascinating world that whetted my appetite to be a professional basketball player. He took me to the horse races to watch his own horse. He let me go over to his home any time to borrow records from his enormous jazz collection. He included me with his entourage whenever they went to a jazz club in Harlem.

This was a world where no one dared call you a nigger. Not to your face.

My mother warned me to be careful not to intrude. "Lewis, Wilt is a grown man with plenty of things to do and people he will want to be seeing alone. He might not want you to come over to his house all the time. He might not want to spend all his time with a boy still in high school." I was the only kid in my high school hanging out with a celebrity, which brought me a little proximity celebrity of my own. Even in summer, word got around. But Mom got me worried that maybe I was nothing more than a kid pestering a kindhearted celebrity. So I told Wilt what my mom said.

"Nah, it's cool, Lewis. Your mother's all right. Make sure you always listen to her. But, no, don't worry about it."

When summer ended, I returned to the demands of school and basketball while Wilt returned to his NBA commitments. But the taste of the sweet life that could be mine stayed with me.

18

Girls and Me and Basketball Make Three

Wilt and I didn't have any of those heart-to-heart talks about the ways of the world or the mysteries of life or the agonies of adolescence. That wasn't his style. He showed me the way life could be, and that was my lesson. Take it or leave it. One of his lessons that never quite took hold was how to deal with girls.

Every time I visited Wilt, there was another beautiful woman. Not only were they gorgeous, but they were friendly, funny, and kind. It would have been easy to dismiss Wilt's success with women as merely the result of his wealth and celebrity, but the women I met seemed to genuinely enjoy his company. He was outgoing and generous, loved to laugh, always knew what to say.... Basically, he was the exact opposite of me.

I tried to copy Wilt's style, to be suave and sophisticated, but I didn't have it in me. I was shy and quiet, and I avoided the spotlight. I was respectful with girls, polite, nonaggressive to the point of never making any move.

One complication to my having a serious dating life was that my fantasy woman was the Italian actress Sophia Loren, famous for her sultry, sensuous looks and curvaceous body. I unfairly compared girls I met against this impossible paragon and was disappointed that none measured up. Of course, it's natural for teenage boys and girls to look for their romantic ideals in media idols like singers or movie stars, but what I began to realize was that my model was a woman with Caucasian features. *Why was that?* Part of the problem was not having many famous black movie stars whom young black teens could admire. The American ideal of beauty was white, and I had been brainwashed into it. When I came to that realization, I felt both ashamed I hadn't realized it earlier and free to appreciate the beauty beyond the glossy covers of popular magazines.

That realization led to another. Whenever I watched my beloved Westerns growing up, I had always rooted for the cavalry to defeat the savage Indians (even though my mother was part Cherokee). *But why was that?* African Americans had much more in common with the Indians than with the soldiers. I remember watching *Distant Drums* with Gary Cooper and rooting for him to wipe out those nasty Seminole Indians. But my summer at HARYOU learning about black history led me to discover that the Seminoles also had a significant population of free black people and runaway slaves they called Black Seminoles. I had been rooting against my own people.

I dated Sandy from HARYOU a few more times after that evening at the Latin Quarter with Wilt. Sandy's uncle was Babs Gonzales, a well-known jazz vocalist. She told me that he had been born Lee Brown but changed his name to Ricardo Gonzales so he could pass for Mexican and get hotel rooms that were denied to black people. It was strange to me that here was yet another person who had changed his name to reinvent himself. Although Sandy and I shared a love for jazz, I just didn't have enough time left over after studies and basketball to keep dating her.

Based on the tales they told, all my friends were wildly successful with girls. According to them, they were doing things I'd only seen James Bond do in the movies. They happily shared their romance wisdom with me: Treat them badly, let them know who's boss, keep them guessing whether you care or not. It was hard to argue with their success, but I knew that I didn't want to be that kind of person. It wasn't how my dad treated my mom. I knew what it felt like to be treated as less, to be belittled. I would have to plug along playing at romance the way I played at hearts: with a losing hand.

Then I met Cheri Benoit.

She was a year younger, very pretty, very outspoken. I liked her immediately, and for some reason I couldn't fathom, she liked me, too.

Cheri and I saw each other as regularly as we could, given my busy schedule, but we told no one. I didn't want to get caught up in the usual high school gossip about who was seeing whom. Anything you cared about could be used against you. The downside was that since no one knew we were seeing each other, my friend Kelly one day started telling me how he was putting the romantic moves on Cheri. I didn't let on, but as he gave me the juicy details, I felt my anger rise. After that, I stopped talking to Cheri for six months. I missed her, but I was so disappointed that she preferred Kelly to me that I couldn't face her.

Whenever I saw her, I managed to sneak away before she could see me. I was constantly on the lookout just so I could avoid her. Then, one day, I turned around and there she was, standing in front of me with a scowl. She pulled me aside. "What happened to you, Lew?"

I didn't know what to say.

"You hurt me, you know that? You didn't call or anything."

"I know."

"And don't think I didn't see you running off every time I came near."

But why was I feeling guilty? She was the one who had wronged me. "I wasn't trying to be mean. It's just that when Kelly told me about you and him—"

"Me and Kelly?" she interrupted. "I talked to Kelly, but that's it. Just talked."

Cheri taught me a valuable lesson about the foolishness of male pride. I had lost six months of time with her based on some boyish bragging, without even talking to her about it. After our talk, Cheri and I continued to date until I went off to California for college and she went to Pennsylvania. We started to see each other again on and off during college and even when I was in the NBA. We never could quite make the romance work in the long term, but we did succeed at friendship, and I would occasionally visit her and her husband when I was in New York years later.

Hanging out with Wilt so much that summer, and seeing how he owned every room he entered, how he was loved by the public, and how successful he was with women, had made me envy him. But I wasn't him. As much as I enjoyed my glimpse into his glitzy and energetic lifestyle, I couldn't help but wonder what other parts of his life might not be right for me.

19

Senior Year: We Gotta Get Out of This Place

My senior year was the part of a roller-coaster ride when you slowly—agonizingly slowly—climb the lift hill, hearing each link clack into place as you rise, eagerly anticipating reaching the top and swooshing straight down. The whole year was a boring repeat of the year before, with all my focus being on the sweet day when I would burst off to college, never to look back.

My social life that year mostly consisted of hanging with my small group of friends. We called ourselves the Colleagues, which we thought was cool and sophisticated, but it now sounds like a cross between a Harvard law club and a frat house folk-singing group. Our main activities were visiting jazz clubs and throwing parties.

Jazz had become the soundtrack to my life story. I used it to explore my emotions, to lift me up when I was down, to mellow me out when I was anxious. Some of the clubs we went to were the same ones that I had visited with Wilt, but now, without him and his spotlight, the clubs felt more personal and intimate. Without the attention, I could just enjoy the music. I listened to, and even met, some of the greatest jazz musicians in the world: Roland Kirk, Sonny Rollins, and Thelonious Monk. Soon I became so inspired that I began to take saxophone lessons.

The Colleagues didn't just sit passively and listen to music; we rented spaces and threw large parties that drew a couple of hundred people. We provided the place, the records, and the punch, and charged only ninety-nine cents because anything a dollar up meant paying city taxes. Kids danced and socialized and let loose while we divvied up a few bucks of profit. We were the kings of the local underground social world.

My parents had loosened the reins slightly since I was doing so well academically and athletically, and I still attended Mass every Sunday, so they knew nothing of the

Circa 1950–51. My mother, Cora, gazes at me in admiration of my remarkable resemblance to a real cowboy. I'm three or four here and in the early stages of my obsession with Western lore.

Circa 1950. Mom was a fantastic seamstress. Here she is working on a happy customer's wedding dress at Alexander's Department Store.

1952. Me and my big ears at Public School 52. I'm only five years old and already the biggest kid in the class.

1955. I made third grade look classy.

1956. Fourth-grade basketball looks a little chaotic here. The other two players seem more like they're practicing dance steps than playing.

1956. At Holy Providence in Cornwells Heights, Pennsylvania, I was able to see over the heads of the rest of my fourth-grade class.

Circa 1957–58. I'm in fifth or sixth grade, and my father snaps a photo of me modeling my St. Jude gym uniform. Maybe I'm also screwing in a light bulb on the ceiling.

Circa 1958–59. I'm feeling confident in my Inwood Little League uniform. Back then, I dreamed of playing professional baseball, not basketball.

1958. I'm in sixth grade, wielding a Native American tomahawk. My dad, Ferdinand, clearly doesn't share my enthusiasm.

Mom and me that same evening. As usual, she's in a better mood than Dad.

1960. In eighth grade, I was six foot eight. It was like an R. L. Stine Goosebumps story, *The Incredible (Well-Dressed) Stretching Kid.*

1964. Mom and me when I was seventeen and looking like a jazz musician.

Dad and me that same day in 1964. Dad looks like he's trying to stand as tall as humanly possible.

1964. My teammates and I at Power Memorial celebrate a hard-fought victory over rivals at DeMatha High School. I was seventeen and in eleventh grade, looking forward to playing even better in my senior year.

1964. Carl Green, Sandy Caseles, me, and Wilt Chamberlain at The Copacabana, the hottest nightclub in New York City. Wilt, the most famous basketball player of the time, insisted on showing me and my date, Sandy, the lifestyle of the rich and famous.

1965. Coach Jack Donahue and me at a school assembly. My removed demeanor shows our chilly relationship after he'd used the N-word with me.

1965. My senior year of high school, sitting in Russian History class. The expression on my face tells the story: I had already agreed to go to UCLA, and I was just marking time until I was on a plane to California.

1965. I'm just about to jam a dunk through the hoop. It's kind of a showy shot, but very satisfying when the hoop rattles, almost like a cheer.

1966. My freshman season, playing against Allan Hancock College in the brand-new Pauley Pavilion.

1966. Me and my first Mercedes. The car was gorgeous, and I look a little scared to drive it, no doubt worried about scratching it.

© David Hume Kennerly/Getty Images

1966. In the UCLA versus Oregon game, all three of us—Mike Nicksic from the University of Oregon, Mike Warren from UCLA, and I—are jumping pretty high. But my long arms gave me a definite advantage in snagging the ball.

Circa 1967–68. Muhammad Ali and me fooling around at a party in Los Angeles my freshman year at UCLA. I couldn't control my smiling because the Champ was hanging out with me. Fortunately, there are no audio recordings of what we sounded like.

Howard Bingum

June 1967. Bill Russell, Muhammad Ali, and I pose at the Cleveland Summit. I was only twenty, the youngest member of the group, and I felt both honor and a great sense of responsibility. Despite the serious occasion, Ali was still mugging for the camera, jokingly extolling his virtues. The original caption for this photo is especially interesting, because despite his having changed his name to Muhammad Ali three years earlier, the reporter insisted on referring to him as Cassius Clay: "Dwarfed by Bill Russell (left), six-foot, 11-inch player coach of the Boston Celtics, and 7-foot, 3-inch college star Lew Alcindor, Cassius Clay strains his neck as he talks with the two basketball giants. A group of the nation's top athletes met to hear Clay's views for rejecting Army induction. *Ring Magazine*, a boxing publication, announced June 5th that it would continue to recognize Clay as the heavyweight champion despite the actions of the World Boxing Association and the New York Athletic Commission in stripping Clay of the title."

1967. Muhammad Ali and his entourage congratulate me after a UCLA victory over Loyola University.

1967. Coach John Wooden and I celebrate UCLA winning the NCAA National Championship over Dayton. This was my first win but Coach's third. I guess he should have been wearing the net.

1967. My sophomore year and I was on the cover of *Sports Illustrated* again. I'm staring at the ball as if it were a crystal ball telling me my future. Maybe it was.

1968. Once again showing the world the latest fashion accessory, the game net, after winning the NCAA National Championship by defeating North Carolina.

March 22, 1968. The press dubbed this matchup between UCLA and Houston the Game of the Century. I'm launching into my famous skyhook while UCLA forward Mike Lynn (35), guard Lucius Allen (42), and Houston forward Elvin Hayes (44), forward/center Ken Spain (14), and guard Don Chaney (24) look on. We defeated Houston 101–69, sending us to the finals against North Carolina. I was named MVP for the tournament.

1969. Here I am at twenty-two, with a cover story in *Sports Illustrated* and starting my career as a professional basketball player with the Milwaukee Bucks. I wore the dashiki to show my pride in my African heritage, something black people were only beginning to do at that time.

1972. Bruce Lee spars with me on the set of *Game of Death*. Bruce died during filming, after my footage was already shot. He was my martial arts teacher and a good friend whose lessons still stay with me today.

1973. I was playing for the Milwaukee Bucks, and becoming more comfortable with my conversion to Islam.

Colleagues, the parties, or the nightly visits to jazz clubs. I was living a separate life from the polite Good Boy Lew that teachers and parents raved about.

The basketball season that year was déjà vu. We won. A lot. Seventy-one games in a row. In fact, we hadn't lost a game since I was a freshman. Coach drove the team with even more intensity, though I did notice that he backed off me a little after our confrontation. He couldn't help but notice my lackluster appearance at his basketball camp. Whatever relationship we had before was over.

After seventy-one victories, we found ourselves facing DeMatha again. The last time we'd played them was the day after Coach Donahue had called me a nigger—and we had beaten them with a fury. I had wondered that night if my teammates had played with extra ferocity as a show of support for me after what Coach had said. I would have been too embarrassed to ask them, but ever since that shattering night, we seemed to bond together much more, both on and off the court. We played with almost mystic unity, as if we were the fingers of the same hand.

On this night, DeMatha came prepared for us. They had two big men, Bob Whitmore and Sid Catlett, both six foot eight. Bob would later be drafted by the Boston Celtics, and Sid would play for the Cincinnati Royals. Their guard, Bernie Williams, would play for the San Diego Rockets. I mention this because so many people think that because I was so tall, winning basketball games was easy. As if all I had to do was stand next to the basket, catch a lob pass, and drop the ball into the hoop. But there were a lot of tall guys out on the court, most thicker and heavier than I was, and they were also fast and agile and talented. The difference in size between me and Bob and Sid was about the length of a crayon. That's an edge, sure, but not enough to make a significant difference unless you also have playing skills and a highly trained team.

The game took place at the University of Maryland field house, which was filled to its fourteen-thousand-seat capacity. We played hard, but with me being double- and triple-teamed during the whole game, we struggled. We kept it close, but in the end we were beaten, 46–43. Our streak ended, and we tasted the bitterness of defeat for the first time in three years. My teammates took the loss pretty well. There had been a lot of pressure on each of us not to lose after seventy-one games, so in a small way, losing was a little bit of a relief. Not for me, though. While my teammates changed and chatted, I sat in the locker room, still in my uniform, replaying the whole game in my head. I had scored only sixteen points, a career low for me. The last time we played them, I had scored thirty-five points. We'd lost by only three points. One play could have turned it around. What if I had taken that shot instead of passing it? What if I'd gotten that rebound I'd missed? I couldn't help but blame myself.

Coach Donahue noticed my morose mood. "What's going on, Lew?"

"Nothing," I said. I wasn't thinking of our personal tensions right then. I was thinking about the game. About all the what-ifs.

"Doesn't look like nothing," he said.

I looked up at him. He seemed remarkably calm considering we had just lost and how much he hated losing. His winning streak as a coach was also broken.

"I should have played better," I said softly.

"Did you play your hardest?"

"Yes."

"Did your teammates play their hardest? Is there someone in this locker room who let us down?" He looked at the other guys as if I was supposed to point someone out.

I shook my head. "It wasn't them."

"Now wait a minute, Lew," he said. "You're saying that you single-handedly lost the game?"

I didn't respond. I could sense a trap.

"Don't you think that's kind of selfish? Because that implies that you must have single-handedly won all the other games. Isn't that right? Are you willing to take credit for winning all seventy-one games? Yes or no?"

I didn't say anything. I knew he was trying to comfort me, but I wasn't willing to accept his comfort.

"Listen up, boys," he continued, addressing all of us. "I'm the coach. If I blamed myself for this loss, then I also have to take credit every time we won. I'd have to assume it was my brilliant coaching, not your playing, that was responsible. But we all know that's not true."

The team stood perfectly still while he spoke.

"This is the finest high school basketball team in the country, maybe the world. Let that sink in. Being the best isn't just about winning games. . . . It's about how you act when you don't win a game."

On one level, I appreciated Coach's speech. We weren't suddenly happy, but he had relieved some of the burden. But on another level, I resented his trying to make me feel better, because that meant he still had the power to make me feel bad or good. Could I ever be sure he wouldn't call me nigger again if he thought that would motivate me? I had to make sure that I didn't give anyone that power. I had learned that much from my time with Wilt, who seemed vulnerable to no one. Wilt owned every room he entered, every court he stepped onto. It seemed to me that no one could hurt him, and that's how I wanted to be.

We never lost another game. By spring, we were chosen national champions for the second year in a row. Stories about our team appeared in national publications. We were local heroes. Coach Donahue was a local hero.

I enjoyed winning for my team's sake and my sake, but it still bothered me that our triumphs were shared by Coach Donahue and Power Memorial. It was endurable only because I knew that in a few months I'd be gone forever.

20

Choosing a College

Senior year at Power followed a predictable routine I had long ago mastered. I gave the teachers what they wanted, and in return I got what I wanted: straight As. I had my eyes on the enormous changes going on in the world outside our school, but I stopped trying to change anyone's minds inside it. I had recently read James Baldwin's essays in *Notes of a Native Son*, after having read his *The Fire Next Time* in eighth grade and being deeply affected by its bluntness about race relations in America. Baldwin wrote, "Do I really want to be integrated into a burning house?" To me at that time, Power Memorial Academy represented America's patriarchal racist past, and that patriarchal system was already burning itself up by trying to stop the inevitable change going on. I was looking to the future—a future described in the

Constitution, where everyone was treated equally. The first step in my joining that future was finding the right college.

My main focus in senior year was trying to decide which college was the best one for me. Basketball scholarship offers were flooding in daily, so I could go to any school I wanted. I just had to narrow down what I was looking for. But I had a lot of requirements. Whatever school I selected would be a showcase for my playing, which would determine my professional basketball career. Being on a winning team would position me to get a well-paying contract. Being on a losing team would make me less valuable. The wrong choice could cost me millions of dollars in the long run. But winning wasn't my only criterion for basketball; I also wanted to play under a coach who treated his players with respect and dignity.

But my choice wasn't based on basketball alone—I was also interested in strong academics. I knew that the career of an athlete, whether in college or in the pros, depended on avoiding serious injuries, so I needed to study and make sure I had a degree I could use in case basketball didn't last. Even more important, I loved to learn. My passion for history and writing had been reignited, and I was eager to take my education to the next step at a university level where teachers wouldn't be hiding the faces of important histori-cal people. As much as I daydreamed about winning college basketball games in front of huge crowds of cheering fans, I also dreamed of all the books I would be reading, the intense discussions of politics and literature in classes. I wanted both.

But mostly I wanted to get away from home. To see what kind of man I would grow into outside the stifling shadow of my father and emotional grip of my mother.

After visiting North Carolina and seeing the way they treated civil rights marchers, I knew I didn't want to attend any school in the South. After much discussion between Coach, my parents, and me, I narrowed down my choices to the University of Michigan, Columbia University, St. John's University, and UCLA.

I went back and forth among the four schools, driving myself crazy trying to make up my mind. Finally, I decided to visit the UCLA campus, after which I would choose once and for all.

21

California: A Brand-New Me

The hot California sun glinted off the shiny metal roofs of the World War II Quonset huts. *This can't be the right place*, I thought, stopping in my tracks. The great basketball coach, John Wooden, who had just taken his team to back-to-back national championships, couldn't possibly have his office in this collection of shabby buildings that looked like an abandoned army camp. Not at one of the most prestigious campuses in the country. If this was how they treated their famous basketball coach, how much worse would it be for the team? Were they going to pitch a tent for us to live in? Had I just flown three thousand miles for nothing?

On the other hand...

I had just hiked across the greenest expanse of grass I had ever seen, under the brightest sun I had ever seen, among the most attractive coeds I had ever seen. For a seventeen-year-old high school kid hopped up on hormones and hubris, this was a lot to take in. Even when I had traveled outside New York City, I'd usually done so in a battered old school bus and only went from smelly gymnasium to smelly gymnasium. With that in mind, the metal huts weren't so bad at all.

I knocked on the door and heard a pleasant voice say, "Come in."

A friendly looking man in a blinding white shirt and midnight-black tie stuck out his hand when I walked in. "Welcome, Lewis," John Wooden said. He was only five foot ten, short for a former basketball star. But during a forty-six-game stretch, he had sunk 134 consecutive free throws. He knew his way around a court, both on the boards and from the sidelines.

I'd expected to be intimidated by Coach Wooden, but I surprised myself by being pretty calm. Instead, I felt impatient to finish all this agonizing over which college to attend and eager for my college life to actually start. I wanted to challenge myself against the best college players to see how good I could become. I wanted to attend classes with renowned scholars. I wanted to date cute girls.

He gestured for me to sit across from his desk and I did. The top of his desk was filled with papers containing practice drills and player notes from his team. I saw Gail Goodrich's name with some scribbled notes beside it. It took every bit of self-control not to crane my neck around to read what he'd written about one of the greatest college players around. That could be my name next year. What would he write about me? My heart started to beat rapidly with excitement.

I didn't say anything. I didn't know what to ask. I figured he'd quiz me about my game, my playing style, favorite moves.

He gave me a long look through his nerdy black-frame glasses. "I'm impressed with your grades, Lewis," he finally said.

Really? He wanted to talk about grades?

He looked me straight in the eyes to make sure I knew he was serious. "For most students, basketball is temporary. But knowledge is forever."

"Yes, sir," I said.

"You can only play basketball for so long, then you've got to get on with the rest of your life."

I nodded.

"My players graduate with good grades. If they choose to

continue to play basketball, that's great. But if they don't or can't, they then have the education to choose another path. That's why you're in college in the first place. To give yourself choices."

That was unexpected. I had visited many other colleges and universities, and their coaches had mostly flattered me while hard-selling their sports programs that would bring me glory and national adulation. This was the first coach to emphasize academics over athletics. He was more concerned about our long-term happiness than our win-loss record. He didn't treat me as a basketball player, but as a student who would be playing basketball on the side.

We talked for about thirty minutes, only briefly touching on basketball. He told me that most often he recruited players for quickness rather than size and had never coached someone as tall as I was, but added, "I'm sure we will find the proper way to use you on the court. I am looking forward to coaching someone like you."

We stood and shook hands again.

"Freshman year can be very difficult," he warned. "Making that transition from high school isn't easy. There are a lot of adjustments, especially for athletes, who have to train every day for several hours."

I nodded again.

He smiled. "But you seem like the kind of young man up to the challenge."

The challenge. That's what I was looking for in a school, and somehow he knew that. Rather than tell me how easily I would fit in and how smoothly everything would go, he appealed to the competitor in me.

I flew back home to my box full of scholarship offers, but I was pretty sure that UCLA would be my new home. First, though, I had to have my parents' final approval.

A few weeks later, Coach Wooden and his assistant coach Jerry Norman arrived at our two-bedroom apartment on Nagle Avenue, in the Dyckman Houses. Two white guys in sports jackets and ties knocking on a door in the housing project usually meant bad news. Not this time. Despite all the offers, Coach Wooden was the only one my parents had invited to our home. They knew I had my heart set on UCLA, and they wanted to make sure they could trust these men with their seven-foot baby.

My dad studied the men with his cop's X-ray vision, sizing up their character the way he would a perp at a crime scene. My mom smiled pleasantly, but her eyes were just as probing as Dad's. Right now, they didn't care about scholarship money or UCLA's reputation—they were measuring the men who would be, on some level, replacing them for the next four years. My parents expected them to look out for me.

"Lewis," my mom said, "why don't you go wait in your room while we talk."

I gave her an annoyed look, but she just stared back. This was my future. I didn't want to wait in my room like some romance novel heroine whose parents were arranging her marriage. This was the reason I had to get as far away from here as I could. As far away as California.

For the next hour, I strained to listen through the walls to what they were saying. My ear was rubbed raw from being pressed against the rough wall. Finally, my mom hollered, "Lewis, come say good-bye."

I stepped out of my room into the living room. Everyone was smiling so I felt encouraged. "Thank you for coming," I said to the coaches and shook their hands.

When they were gone, I turned anxiously to my parents. I was determined to go, with or without their blessing. But with would be much easier.

"That Coach Wooden," my father said.

Holding my breath, I waited for him to go on.

"He's very dignified."

"A gentleman," my mom agreed. "Not the kind of man who'd take advantage of you." She was worried that a school might try to exploit me. Coach Wooden had assured them he would look out for me, and they believed him.

My parents must have made an impression on him, too. When I announced my decision to attend UCLA at a press conference about a week after his visit, Coach Wooden told the media, "This boy is not only a fine student and a great college basketball prospect, but he is also a refreshingly modest young man who shows the results of excellent parental and high school training.

"After meeting Mr. and Mrs. Alcindor, I could easily understand the fine impression Lew made on all of us when he visited our campus. Their guidance has enabled him to handle the fame and adulation that has come his way in a most gracious and unaffected manner."

When my parents heard that, they were ready to adopt him into the family.

From that day on, my heart was lighter with the knowledge that I was just a few short months from freedom. From Coach Donahue. From my parents. From everything and everyone I knew. I knew I should be a little scared, but I wasn't. I was California dreamin'.

22

My Reunion
with Coach Donahue

It was thirty-five years after the terrible incident with Couch Donahue, the one that had destroyed our close relationship. I had retired from professional basketball and was visiting Coach Wooden at his home. We were watching a baseball game in his cluttered den, which was filled with trophies, photographs of each of his national championship teams, many books, and hand-painted plates signed by his grandchildren.

For no reason I could fathom, Coach Wooden suddenly brought up Coach Donahue. He knew the story, knew how much it had affected me. But that was so long ago that I didn't think he even remembered it. "I don't think I ever told you this story, Kareem," he said. "But I met Jack Donahue back in 1965, before you came to UCLA for your visit. It was right after UCLA had won its first national championship. I was on some local TV show promoting a coaching clinic I was doing in Valley Forge, Pennsylvania. Right after the show, I got a phone call from Jack, and he said he'd like to come down and talk to me about his player, Lew Alcindor."

"Really?" This was news to me.

"Well," Coach said, "he came down and told me that UCLA was one of the four schools you wanted to visit. That was the first contact that we had with you. Did you know that?"

"No," I said.

"Long drive," he said.

I didn't say anything.

"Two and a half hours," he said.

"Has anyone ever accused you of being too subtle?"

He laughed. "Quite the opposite. I'm accused of cranking out neat little sayings that are T-shirt ready."

I laughed, but I was thinking about Jack Donahue leaving his family on a day off to drive five hours for a surly kid who barely talked to him. What kind of man does that, yet never tries to win back the kid's favor by telling him?

"Have you ever made a mistake, Kareem?" he asked me quietly.

Too many to count, I thought.

"I know how easy it is to make a mistake in the heat of competition," he said, "and how hard it is to recover from that mistake."

I looked at Coach Wooden's kind face and thought how, but for that one spontaneous outburst long ago, I might still be visiting Coach Donahue, watching TV with him.

A few years after that conversation, I was again sitting in Coach Wooden's den, this time watching women's basketball, when the phone rang. It was Jack Donahue. He was in Los Angeles and wanted to visit Coach Wooden.

Knowing that Coach Donahue was on the other end of the phone didn't bother me. Since my last conversation with Coach Wooden, I had lost any animosity I'd once had.

"I've got someone here I'd like you to talk to," Coach Wooden said and handed me the phone.

I took it. "Hey, Coach," I said cheerfully. "How are you?"

"Fine, Kareem, fine." I could hear the relief in his voice and I was glad.

We chatted briefly, made arrangements to meet in a

couple of hours, and hung up. I turned to Coach Wooden. "That was some coincidence, him calling you while I was here."

He shrugged, not even bothering to deny he'd arranged the call. "I'm still your coach," he said. "Always will be."

I met Coach Donahue at my home. He apologized again, as he had done to me and in the press when the story came out. Since then, he'd gone on to a distinguished career, including coaching four Canadian Olympic men's basketball teams. It touched me that despite all he had accomplished, he still was bothered by how he'd hurt a seventeen-year-old kid almost forty years earlier.

I told him that I forgave him and that I knew he hadn't been a racist, just unknowingly insensitive. I thanked him for all he had done for me, which he looked grateful to hear.

We parted with a handshake and good feelings toward each other. Eighteen months later, he died of prostate cancer. I attended his memorial, happy that we'd been able to resolve what had happened so long ago. I was also grateful to Coach Wooden, not just for bringing me and Jack Donahue together, but for helping me become the kind of man who could let go of animosity and forgive past hurts.

PART 3

College Daze:
My Years of Living Wondrously

•————————————•

"The paradox of education is precisely this—that as one begins to become conscious one begins to examine the society in which he is being educated."

JAMES BALDWIN

23

Welcome to the Hotel California

My first day in sunny California didn't turn out as sunny as I'd expected.

Maybe I'd expected too much. After all, to everyone growing up on the East Coast in the 1960s, Southern California was a utopia of sun, beaches, movie stars, and a laid-back lifestyle. *Beach Blanket Bingo*, the fifth in a series of beach party movies, had just hit theaters. The Beach Boys' "California Girls" had just been released and seemed to playing nonstop on every radio station. And there was Disneyland, which was the only one in the world at that time! We assumed that the "happiest place on Earth" beamed out all the overflow happiness to the surrounding areas. The rest of the country might have been burning up from civil unrest, but California heat was for toasting on a quiet beach. The perfect place for me to take a deep breath and discover how I fit into the world—as an athlete, as a student, as a man, as an African American.

All summer after committing to UCLA, I acted as if I were a rock star on my farewell tour. I hung out with my buddies, went to jazz clubs, played basketball, even played in the Rucker Tournament for the first time. In my mind, I was already unpacking my suitcase in my UCLA dorm. I tried not to act too excited around my friends because I knew a lot of them were jealous. I could see in their eyes what they were thinking: *California, man...anything is possible out there. Harlem? Not so much.*

Tension between my parents and me had gone to DEF-CON 1. I had taken to staying out later and later until one night I'd come home so late that to escape their yelling I barricaded myself in my room. I dragged my dresser in front of my door while they banged against it and hollered at me about responsibility. I shut them out of my room and my life, imagining myself on a silvery jet plane to Los Angeles. In California, I would finally find out who I was away from the restrictions of parents, Catholic schools, the church, Harlem, and even my friends. All my favorite movies were not about people who start the movie heroic and stay that way—they were about people who started frightened and became brave, started selfish and became generous, started weak and became strong.

Then my perfect snow globe version of California cracked.

From August 11 to 16, 1965, a couple of weeks before I arrived, major rioting broke out in the mostly black Watts neighborhood of Los Angeles. Watts exploded into burning, looting, and killings that spread out over a forty-six-square-mile war zone. It all started after a black driver was arrested for drunk driving. A crowd gathered, the arrested man's family interjected, and a fight broke out. The incident itself wasn't the issue—the community's reaction was incited by what they saw as decades of institutional racism and police brutality. The result was that four thousand members of the California National Guard were inserted into the area to stop the rioting. When it finally ended, there were thirty-four dead and more than $40 million in property damage.

I now realized that there was no place for me to take a step back from what was going on. It was happening everywhere. Watts was only thirty miles from UCLA. Wherever

I went, I would have to confront the racial issues flaring up all over the country. But I was only eighteen. I wanted to study, play basketball, meet girls, act a little crazy, and figure out who I was and what I wanted to do with my life, just like all the white kids got the chance to do. But I had to drag along the additional baggage of race. I thought I'd be able to leave that behind in New York, just for a little while. Watts changed that. Even here under the cheerful sun, I realized I would still be a symbol of all black people, a spokesperson for the black causes, an information kiosk for the curious, and a target for vitriol and violence from the ignorant.

I walked into my dormitory that first day a little disheartened. As I strolled down the hall to my dorm room, ducking through doorways, students openly stopped and stared at me. I was used to that reaction by now, but I had expected college students in California to be cooler, with less gawking.

To be fair, the school newspaper had made a big deal of my attending, and plenty of students who saw me that first day offered friendly greetings of "Welcome to LA, man" and "Go Bruins!" But being the guy they were heaping team victory expectations on was isolating. I just wanted to be accepted as a regular student.

That first day, I decided I'd had enough of being stared at and whispered about, so I marched straight to my dorm room, turned out the light, and went to sleep. My first Saturday night in California wasn't exactly the giddy celebration I had envisioned all summer.

The next morning, I was awakened by a ringing phone. I answered with a groggy hello.

"Mr. Alcindor?" the voice prompted.

"Uh-huh." I yawned, still dazed from jet lag.

"I was told to give you directions to the Newman Center."

"The Newman Center?" I yawned again.

"That's where they have Catholic Mass. If you hurry, you can still make it."

I didn't say anything.

"You're Catholic, right?"

"Newman Center. Mass. Got it. Thanks a lot." I hung up and pulled the covers back over my head.

That was the first Sunday in my life that I deliberately skipped Mass. I never went again. The California Lew Alcindor chose his own beliefs. He wasn't sure yet what they were, but he knew what they weren't.

I felt a little guilty for my mother's sake. She would be

disappointed, and I hated to disappoint people. New York Lew Alcindor was nothing if not a people pleaser, a Good Boy who any young woman would be proud to take home to Mama.

Was that who California Lew Alcindor was, too? I'd have to wait and see.

Official basketball practice hadn't started yet, but I wanted to stay sharp, so I walked over to the gym with my roommate, Lucius Allen, a high school All-American guard from Kansas City. We'd chatted in our room about typical subjects: girls, basketball, girls, school, girls. We hadn't yet seen each other play, so today was going to be an audition for both of us.

When we arrived, a couple of other freshmen were already there, along with four varsity players. We quickly divided into two teams, freshmen versus varsity. Since they were part of the reigning national championship team, the varsity players probably thought this would be a good opportunity to establish the team pecking order.

We beat them three games in a row.

I left feeling pretty good about our freshman team.

Life Outside Basketball

On the basketball court, I felt confident in my skills and I trusted the coaches, so I did everything they told me to do. That part of my life was smooth and predictable. It was the rest of campus life that gave me problems. I was still shy and socially awkward when it came to interacting with other students.

One place I felt the same confidence as on the basketball court was in the classroom. At first, teachers treated me like the typical dumb jock, not expecting me to participate much in classroom discussions or to raise my hand to answer tough questions. I surprised them all by taking my schoolwork as seriously as I did my sports.

It was in my English Composition class that I discovered a love that rivaled my devotion to basketball. Professor

Lindstrom assigned us to write a descriptive essay about anything. "Anything at all," he'd encouraged. "But hopefully something that matters to you in some way." I sat in my dorm room that night nervously gnawing the end of my pen as I struggled to think of a topic. What mattered to me? Basketball? I was sick of talking about that with anyone except guys on the team. School? I'm sure half the class would be writing about how hard it was adjusting to college life. Civil rights? Important, but too broad and preachy. I wanted something about me. As I dug through every corner of my brain for a good topic, I realized I had the John Coltrane album *My Favorite Things* playing in the background.

I started writing.

I wrote about the Village Vanguard, my favorite jazz club in New York. I described the descent into the basement where the walls were checkerboarded with photos of jazz greats who had played there, like Miles Davis, Thelonious Monk, Charlie Parker, and Sonny Rollins. At the end of the tunnel-like room was the spotlighted stage, backed by a red curtain, where the owners, Max and Lorraine Gordon, would introduce Stan Getz, Anita O'Day, the Modern Jazz Quartet, and many other jazz performers, known and unknown. That was the physical place, but what I wanted to convey was how it felt to sit at one of the small round tables on a stiff wooden chair and have the jazz notes burrow inside your brain and chest until you forgot time, despite a parental curfew. And how you're willing to face the wrath of angry parents just to hear one more song.

I turned in my essay, worried that the ramblings of a black kid about jazz in a dark New York City basement club might seem too foreign under the harsh sun of California. But Professor Lindstrom selected my essay to be read and analyzed by the entire class. I felt so excited, not just because he had praised my writing style, but because the subject matter of my life and my observations seemed worthwhile to others. I had the same reaction as the day the four of us freshmen beat the varsity players in our informal scrimmage.

Like I knew what I was doing. Like I belonged here.

That feeling of belonging was reinforced by my many friends on the basketball team. We worked hard every day for hours, traveled together, and shared the adrenaline rush of competition. It was harder for me to make friends off the team, but one friend I did make became my closest.

Jimmy Johnson was an upperclassman from South Central Los Angeles, the heart of the black ghetto. He was a straight-A student with a passion for poetry, jazz, and the kind of in-depth political debates that I had come to college for. We discussed the civil rights movement, what being black meant to us personally, how much we had to teach ourselves about our own culture because we hadn't been brought up learning about it. We knew all about the new black pride movement, which advocated for black people taking pride in their natural looks, African heritage, and fellowship with other black cultures. I'd even let my hair grow out into a short Afro.

My hair symbolized the two very different lives I was leading. In basketball, I followed a very strict regimen of practice and games, practice and games. As a student, I was constantly reaching out to discover new ideas, to figure out what it meant to me. Basketball was all structure, but learning who I was and what I was meant to do was anything but structured.

My freshman year at UCLA was difficult, just as Coach Wooden had warned. Back in New York, I'd had my own room, which had made me the envy of most of my friends. At UCLA, I suddenly was living in a dorm filled with strangers and sharing a tiny room with my teammate Lucius Allen, a bouncy kid with a "golly gee whiz" Midwestern attitude about everything Californian. Definitely not like my boys from uptown back in New York. But, truth be told, there was something endearing about him. His unselfconscious enthusiasm was contagious. We became good friends and eventually played together for both the Milwaukee Bucks and the Los Angeles Lakers.

I quickly discovered that athletes were treated like movie stars at UCLA. But there was a hollowness to that fame, because most of us were broke. My scholarship entitled me to tuition and room and board, but it barely covered living expenses. Edgar Lacey, Lucius Allen, and I had come to UCLA with big reputations, but nothing much in our pockets. We'd chosen UCLA for our futures, but that didn't make the present any easier. We were all cash-poor almost all the time. Worse, we were surrounded by students who were flush, children of wealthy celebrities and business moguls who drove BMWs to their parents' Malibu homes. We barely could afford to go out on a date. We were part of a program that was earning millions of dollars for the university, yet I was literally wearing pants with holes in the pockets.

I never discussed my unhappiness with Coach Wooden.

We hadn't yet developed that type of relationship. I was on my own, shedding at least part of the identity that my parents had worked so hard to instill. And I hadn't yet figured out what to replace it with.

So I turned to basketball. I always knew exactly who I was and what was expected of me on the court.

25

My First Day
with Coach Wooden

John Wooden stood in front of the greatest freshman team in the history of basketball. We sat on the UCLA bench awaiting the first words of wisdom from the world-famous coach we had come from all parts of the country to follow. Some, like me, had turned down full scholarships at other schools just to learn at the feet of the great John Wooden.

"Good morning, gentlemen," Coach Wooden began dryly.

"Good morning, Coach," we chorused.

He looked at us all pleasantly and cleared his throat in preparation to speak.

We leaned forward, ready to tattoo his wisdom on our brains for eternity.

"Today, we are going to learn how to put on our socks and sneakers correctly."

Although we didn't dare snicker, we did look at one another and wonder what the punch line to the joke was.

He bent down and took off his shoes and socks. His pale pink feet looked as if they'd never been exposed to light before. "We are going to talk about tug and snug," he said. "Tug. And. Snug."

The 1965–66 freshman basketball team sitting on that bench included five high school All-Americans. I had graduated from Power Memorial in New York as the most highly recruited player in the country. My college roommate, Lucius, was already considered the best young player to come out of Kansas. Lynn Shackelford from Burbank, California, was an extraordinary shooter, and Kenny Heitz, from Santa Maria, California, was a confident, polished forward. Our fifth starter was Kent Taylor, a walk-on from Texas who later transferred to Houston. We had come to UCLA because it was the best college basketball program in the country—the perfect place for us to fully develop our talent before graduating to professional basketball. The Bruins had won two consecutive national championships during my junior and senior years in high school and were the pre-season favorite to win a third during my freshman season, although they would have to do it without me, Shack, and Kenny, as NCAA rules forbade freshmen from playing varsity basketball. We knew how much raw basketball talent and potential was sitting on this bench, eager to be molded by the great John Wooden.

But was this really the great John Wooden?

Snug-and-Tug Wooden?

We knew what he had accomplished, we knew that his program had produced great basketball players, and we were excited to learn from him. But these were the first minutes of the first day of our four-year college career. We were anxious to begin learning the techniques that had turned UCLA into a championship program.

Was snug and tug the secret to UCLA's success?

He grinned at our puzzled faces. "As Benjamin Franklin said, 'For want of a nail,'" he said, which only made us more puzzled. He sighed and recited:

> *For want of a nail the shoe was lost,*
> *For want of a shoe the horse was lost,*

For want of a horse the rider was lost,
For want of a rider the battle was lost,
For want of a battle the kingdom was lost,
And all for the want of a horseshoe nail.

He shrugged. "You want to learn about basketball, read Benjamin Franklin."

The greatest team in the history of basketball just stared.

"If you do not pull your socks on tightly," he said firmly, "you're likely to get wrinkles in them. Wrinkles cause blisters. Blisters force players to sit on the sideline. And players sitting on the sideline lose games. So we are not just going to tug. We are going to also make it snug."

He demonstrated. We copied what he did.

When we were done, he smiled.

We had entered the gym confident bordering on cocky and just gotten our first lesson in humility from Coach Wooden. We knew that lots of teams started strong in a season, only to succumb to player injuries and drop out of the running. Any injury that kept you from playing hurt the whole team. It was that kind of attention to detail that helped make John Wooden the greatest coach in college basketball history.

None of us ever missed a practice or a game because of a blister.

"I don't drink and I don't smoke," he began again, "and the only reason you have to be up beyond nine or ten o'clock at night is if you're studying." His Hoosier accent gave his words a nasal tone, but the intensity of his look gave the words biblical importance. "Number one in your life is your family. Number two is the religion of your choice. Number three is your studies; you're here to get an education. Number four is to never forget that you represent this great university wherever you are, whatever you are doing. And number five, if we have some time left over, we'll play some basketball." He raised his eyebrows. "Questions?"

There were none.

That first meeting made me ask myself, *What exactly did I hope to learn from Coach Wooden?* I wanted him to somehow translate my relentless desire to be a great player, and my hope to surpass even my own expectations, into practical skills. Ball handling, shooting, setting picks, moving without the ball, teamwork. Check, check, and check. But there was something more that I wanted, something I couldn't articulate. I wanted the game to make sense to my life in a way that was beyond just having a skill set. I wouldn't expect him to understand what I meant. He was old, an ancient fifty-five. He couldn't possibly get what was going on inside a young eighteen–year–old guy like me.

He wouldn't get the chance because my freshman team was coached by Gary Cunningham, so Coach Wooden, who focused on the varsity team, didn't have too much to do with us. But we practiced each afternoon at the same time that the varsity did, with the gym separated by a large curtain.

"Why the curtain?" my roommate asked me one day as we ran warm-up laps.

"I don't know," I said. "Maybe he doesn't want them to see us and pick up bad habits."

"You mean like your turtle speed?" And he burst ahead of me. I ran after him. I was pretty fast for my size, but no one was as fast as Lucius.

At times, I would look and see Coach Wooden peeking around that curtain, just standing there watching us. Some of the guys would pick up their game when they knew he was watching, in an effort to impress him. I didn't change my play because I always played as hard as I could. My parents had instilled in me a disciplined work ethic that dictated I always try to work harder than anyone else in the room. I'd look over and see him studying us as if he were waiting for eggs to hatch, but it didn't make me nervous as it did some of the others. I was confident. Things were already going the way I wanted them to go.

Besides, I was studying him as hard as he was studying us. I respected his reputation, but this was four years of my life we were talking about, and whatever professional career I hoped to have afterward. I had to make sure that he wasn't a million dollars of promise worth ten cents on delivery. It wasn't arrogance but self-preservation, survival. This was the only shot I would get at proving myself to the pros, and I had to make it count.

Sometimes Coach Wooden would call over Coach Cunningham, give him some names, and a few of us would be sent over to work out with the varsity team. In part, he was helping us develop our skills, but he was also giving us a taste of what we could expect if we stuck it out. We would be playing on an elite team that already moved with balletic precision but struck with SWAT-like force.

Practices were highly structured, scheduled to the minute, to the second, to the nanosecond. We knew that he spent two hours every morning just working out the schedule for that day's two-hour practice. He wrote everything down on three-by-five-inch index cards and kept a loose-leaf notebook with detailed notes of every practice session. Most other coaches would simply have pulled out their familiar list of drills that they used every year with every team, but Coach's philosophy was that teams were much more fluid. Other coaches saw their teams as a deck of cards: If one card drops off, you just grabbed another card from the deck. The cards were interchangeable because they only looked at the backs of the cards. Coach Wooden looked at the face values. No two cards were alike just as no two players were alike. He even realized that a player was not the same one day as he was the next. Each time one player progressed or faltered, the whole team's ability was affected.

Sometimes he would climb to the very top level of the Pauley Pavilion and watch us play from up there, where we must have looked like a bunch of beetles scurrying around. Other times he would be courtside, walking along with the players like a shadow.

I had never seen a coach think like that before. I had heard coaches talk about seeing the Big Picture before, but Coach Wooden saw the game in 70 mm Panavision. Yet he saw it on a microscopic level, too.

Every morning he scribbled on those note cards, with drills for the team and customized drills for individuals. I had never met anyone with such an eye for detail and such commitment to his players as names rather than numbers.

Sometimes my teammates and I would laugh a little about how focused he always seemed to be. Secretly, we also felt relief that he took our playing that seriously and wasn't willing to settle for anything less than our best. He saw his job as helping us find out how far we had to go to reach our best. Turned out it was farther away than any of us imagined. And a lot harder to get to.

Yes, he was driven to be the best coach possible, but he had no inclination to be our fatherly friend. He was our coach, and that meant he had a responsibility to each of us—a responsibility that was more a calling than a job. He dressed like a barnstorming Midwestern evangelical preacher, and he had the fervor for making us not just good players but good men. You can't shepherd impressionable boys for four years without changing them.

But as a freshman, all I cared about at first was that game we would play against the varsity team to inaugurate the new thirteen-thousand-seat Pauley Pavilion. Coach Cunningham had planted the seed in my mind during my visit to UCLA, and I was eager to see how we would do against the team that had just won two national championships and was favored to win again this year.

On November 27, 1965, game day finally arrived.

I'd played in front of large crowds before, but this was different. I had been brought here to help win national championships for the three years I could play varsity. There was definitely a "let's see what the kid can do" vibe in the air. I was expected to prove myself, to convince them that they hadn't made a mistake. We were expected to lose, so there would be no shame in that, but if we lost big, I thought I would be blamed. I had to keep reminding myself to breathe.

"Let's go, Turtle," Lucius said, brushing by me as we took the court. "Try to keep up."

"Look for me, Rabbit," I said. "I'll be the one above the rim."

We both grinned, but we could each see the nervousness in the other's face. The only one on our team who looked confident was Coach Cunningham.

In front of a full house of screaming fans, and thousands more watching it live on TV, I took my first shot in Pauley Pavilion...and completely missed the entire basket.

I swallowed something the size of a basketball—my pride, I think—and just pressed on. I didn't miss much after that, piling up thirty-one points. We easily defeated the national champs, 75–60. We could have beaten them by a larger margin, but Coach Cunningham took out our starting team with more than four minutes left. At the party after the game, Coach Wooden was nothing but gracious and congratulatory to the freshman team. He later commented on the game, "It was instantly obvious what Lewis could do and how he could dominate a game."

Although it was an evening of triumph for the team—and vindication for me—I came away with something more. Watching Coach Cunningham's show of respect for Coach Wooden, and seeing Coach Wooden's genial response, planted the seed in me that there truly were more important things than winning: relationships.

26

Meeting Muhammad Ali

One advantage to living in Los Angeles and being a well-known athlete was that I got to meet famous people I admired. The athlete I most admired at that time was the boxing legend Muhammad Ali. He was only five years older but had already made his mark on the world as the youngest person to defeat a heavyweight champion for the title—though he had been stripped of his title for not submitting to being drafted into the army, because, as he explained, "I ain't got nothing against no Viet Cong; no Viet Cong ever called me nigger." Half the world was chanting his name in praise; the other half was sharpening pitchforks and lighting torches to go after the "upstart Negro." To me, he epitomized the athlete with moral integrity and personal courage. The kind of man I hoped one day to become.

When I first met Muhammad Ali, he was performing magic tricks on Hollywood Boulevard. I was a freshman walking down the street with two of my buddies when we saw him strolling along with a small entourage, doing sleight-of-hand illusions for fans who would come up to him. Despite his legal problems with the government and his tumultuous professional career, here he was, casually sauntering down the street as if he hadn't a care in the world. Ali's magic wasn't just the simple tricks he performed, but his ability to draw everyone's attention to him, whether he was in a crowded room or on a busy boulevard. And once he had their attention, he never disappointed them. No matter how many people were around, he was the only one you looked at. He exuded confidence, a sense of purpose, and an undeniable joy.

I shyly approached him to say hello.

"Ah, another big fan of magic," he responded when I greeted him. "And I do mean *big*."

Everyone laughed, including me.

He was friendly and polite and charming...and then he

was gone, moving down the street like a lazy breeze, a steady stream. A force of nature: gentle but unstoppable.

My buddies and I walked away, jabbering giddily about how cool it was to meet the champ, but to me that meeting was much more than running into another celebrity in LA—I'd admired Muhammad Ali since I was thirteen, before he changed his name from Cassius Clay, when he and Rafer Johnson won gold medals in the 1960 Olympics. At that time, the NBA had allowed black players just ten years earlier, and Jackie Robinson had integrated baseball just three years before that. In 1946, the Los Angeles Rams integrated the NFL. So while all eyes were on black athletes to see if they could measure up to white ones, black kids in 1960 didn't yet dare dream of a professional sports career because it was so rare. However, when I watched Rafer and Cassius, I did dream. They were the epitome of the skill, power, and grace of the black athlete, and they inspired me to push myself harder to be such an athlete.

Muhammad Ali's influence on me in those six formative years from when I was thirteen to when I met him on Hollywood Boulevard wasn't just in athletics. Not only had he conquered the boxing world through his undeniable dominance in the ring, but he had mastered the art of self-promotion unlike anyone else. By cannily playing the obnoxious court jester for TV cameras, Muhammad's brash, outrageous antics ensured that Something Would Happen. He bragged relentlessly and shamelessly—and in verse! He riled up white folks so much that they would pay anything to see this uppity young black boy put back in his place. That place, for black people of that time, was wherever they were told to be. Sure, famous athletes and entertainers were invited to sit at the adult table of celebrity, but for everyone else of color, the struggle was still in its infancy. For black people accepted at the adult table, opportunities were limitless. If you were smart and wanted to maintain a successful career, you kept your dark head down and your mouth shut, and occasionally you rhapsodized about how grateful and blessed you felt to be an American.

Not Muhammad Ali.

He was a fighter, whether in or out of the ring. In the ring, he was as much businessman as athlete. Out of the ring, he was a champion of justice. His refusal to submit to the draft during the Vietnam War on the grounds that "my conscience won't let me go shoot my brother, or some darker people" caused him to be sentenced to five years in prison, fined $10,000, and banned from boxing for three years. He didn't fight for three years during his physical prime, when he could have earned millions of dollars, because he stood up for a principle. In 1971, his conviction was overturned by the US Supreme Court in an 8–0 decision, but the damage had already been done.

The next time Muhammad and I met was a few months after our street encounter, at a lavish Los Angeles party mostly attended by college and professional athletes. Members of various UCLA and University of Southern California (USC) teams were there, as were some of the Los Angeles Dodgers. I saw Muhammad floating like a butterfly through the party, flirting with all the women and charming all the men.

Like a typical gawky and insecure freshman, I drifted off on my own to check out the musical instruments the band had abandoned when they took a break. I started quietly hitting the drums, working up a nice beat, when suddenly Muhammad Ali was next to me strumming a guitar. Muhammad's personal photographer, Howard Bingham, immediately swooped in, posed us, and snapped a photograph of us jamming that appeared in *Jet* magazine. When he left, Ali and I sat there alone.

"You sounded pretty good," Ali said to me, nodding at the drumsticks. "You play?"

"Nah, I was just fooling around. My dad's the musician in the family."

"Yeah? Professional?"

"No. He's a cop."

"My dad painted signs." He looked into my eyes. "When I was little, I asked my dad, 'Why can't I be rich?' So he points to my arm, you know, meaning my black skin, and says, 'That's why.'"

I nodded, not sure what to say.

He strummed the guitar once briskly and smiled. "But look at us now, brother."

We grinned at each other, acknowledging our good fortune.

After that evening, Muhammad took on a big-brother role in my life. His influence extended way beyond our connection as athletes. While I admired the athlete of action, it was the man of principle that was truly my role model. He taught me that personal success without community involvement was hollow and meaningless. Championship trophies and plaques and rings were merely building materials to construct a platform to rally people to fix social problems. "When you saw me in the boxing ring fighting, it wasn't just so I could beat my opponent," he explained. "My fighting had a purpose. I had to be successful in order to get people to listen to the things I had to say."

Muhammad Ali was the greatest boxer of his time—some say of all time—but it was his words that carried the most lasting punch. Mostly, he spoke about equality. About raising up people of color to their rightful place. About religious freedom. About ending unjust wars, an unjust draft, an unjust legal system. These were things my friends and I discussed passionately at night in our dorm rooms. But Ali was out there in the real world doing something about it, at great personal cost.

Sometimes he used both his fists and words to make his point. In 1967, when the black fighter Ernie Terrell refused to call Ali by his Muslim name, Ali pummeled Terrell in the eighth round of their fight, shouting, "What's my name? What's my *name*?" That was the moment when I truly understood the significance of his name change. Of course, I understood it intellectually. I had started my own studies into Islam, but to see Ali's face at that moment was to understand what he was really saying: "I named myself. This is the man I choose to be, not the man the world expects me to be."

I'd had plenty of coaches teaching me how to win. Muhammad Ali was the first to teach me what to do with winning.

27

Oh, Yeah, I Also Played Basketball Freshman Year

Although Coach Wooden wasn't technically the coach of the freshman team, he worked closely with Coach Cunningham in preparing me for the three years I would play varsity. Clearly, they were depending on me to continue making the varsity team national champions. They even brought in a special instructor just for me. Former Oregon State player and coach Jay Carty was supposed to increase my mental and physical conditioning. In other words, being big wasn't enough, I had to learn how to *play* big. Carty was six foot eight, 230 pounds, and described himself as a "slow white guy who couldn't jump," but while playing center as a senior at Oregon State, he had continually faced his seven-foot sophomore teammate Mel Counts and learned some moves he wanted to teach me. It was not unusual for teams to hire special coaches for specific players, and the rest of the team was supportive in doing whatever it took for us to win.

Most of the moves involved physically roughing me up on the court so I would be prepared for what I would be facing from meatier, more aggressive players trying to neutralize my height. Jay pummeled me with his knees, elbows, shoulders, and hips until I learned how to counter the abuse with a roll or pivot or some force of my own. We worked on what had become my favorite shot, the elegant hook. Coach Wooden called it the "flat hook" because of the low trajectory. Still, it was effective. But as I added more arc, it became nearly unstoppable.

Coach Wooden's Golden Rule of Basketball—and Life—was one short sentence: "Failing to prepare is preparing to fail." He borrowed that from Ben Franklin, but he made it his own by applying it relentlessly to everything we did. Sometimes he said it loudly and sometimes softly, but he said it often. "Talent comes first," he said. "No one wins without outstanding talent—but not everyone wins with it, either!"

Talent got you to the door; preparedness took you through.

One way he implemented this philosophy was through conditioning. Having just played on a national championship high school team, and being only eighteen, I thought I was already in great shape. He proved me wrong.

"Generally, the team that's in the best shape wins," he would tell us. "You want to know why so many games are won or lost in the last fifteen minutes? Because one team is out of gas and the other team isn't. We're always going to be that other team. Tired players miss more shots, defend less aggressively, snag fewer rebounds. That will *never* be our players."

From the first day of my freshman year until the last practice of my senior year, we ran until we couldn't run anymore. And then we ran some more. There were no shortcuts in John Wooden's basketball program. You did it until you did it right, and then you did it again. That basic philosophy that I learned on those long afternoons enabled me to extend my professional career to twenty years, longer than any other player at that time. I always felt the conditioning regimen I was put through at UCLA was a primary reason I was able to play at a high level in the NBA far longer than players like Wilt Chamberlain. Wilt was dedicated to being stronger than anybody else, but he wasn't able to run the court and he wasn't flexible. As he got older, things that required quickness and agility grew further and further beyond his reach.

Practices usually were scheduled in the afternoon from two thirty to four thirty. After practice I was so exhausted that I would have to go back to my room, collapse onto the bed, and take a nap until nine. Then I'd wake up, do my homework until midnight, and go back to sleep. Not exactly the glamorous lifestyle that fans imagined.

But the hard work paid off. Not just in our victory against the varsity squad, but throughout our entire season. In fact, the varsity team struggled that year with a record of 18–8, the worst in Coach Wooden's last twelve years. Some people blamed their poor season on our demoralizing victory over them, but Coach Wooden emphatically denied that.

Our freshman team did not struggle. We breezed through the season with a 21–0 record, beating other teams by an average of 57 points a game. We beat one college by 103 points, and we won our closest game by 28 points. By the end of the season, we started to see fans waving signs that swapped the UC Los Angeles for "UC Lew Alcindor."

28

The Dinner That Changed My Relationship with Coach Wooden

To celebrate our undefeated season, Coach invited me to dinner for some one-on-one time. We both knew that the fans and the press had a lot of expectations for both of us in the next three years. He had kept me away from the press all year, just as Coach Donahue had, to protect me from being distracted. But that was about to end, and he wanted to make sure I would be able to handle the inevitable criticism that came with the praise.

"The press has made you a hero," he said to me as we

pulled into the parking lot of the restaurant. "And that feels pretty darn good, right?"

"Sure," I said. "I guess." Oh, man, did it ever. Seeing my photo in the newspapers and sports magazines, reading all the great stuff they said about me, that was a dream come true.

"Well, they can make you a villain just as quickly. They don't like something you said, or didn't say. They think you snubbed them or dodged a question...." He shook his head. "They can turn on you."

Coach had faced some criticism and questioning of his own this past season when his team failed to make the NCAA Tournament. Our fortunes were now bound together, and together we would rise or fall over the next three years.

"The thing to remember is that people get tired of reading the same thing about someone. How good they are. How generous. How humble. They want something new." He looked over at me. "Don't give them something new."

"Okay," I said. I wasn't worried. As long as I played my best, what could they say about me?

Coach and I were both huge baseball fans, so he took me to a steak house called the Bat Rack. The owner, Johnny

Sproatt, had decorated the place with baseball bats signed by major league players. We ordered and settled in for some light conversation. Even though the country outside this restaurant was in racial upheaval with riots, murders, and marches, Coach Wooden and I didn't talk race, we talked baseball and basketball. He had carefully constructed a cocoon around his players designed to keep the raging storm outside.

I hadn't made up my mind yet about where Coach stood in all this social upheaval. I liked him. I admired him. And until he did something like Coach Donahue, I would listen to him and do what he advised. And I would eat the steak he was paying for.

After dinner, we stopped in the parking lot to say hello to Johnny Sproatt, who was a major UCLA booster. While we were standing there talking, an elderly white woman came out of the restaurant and just stood there, staring up at me. I was used to people gaping at my height, so I just smiled at her politely.

Finally, she asked Coach Wooden, "How tall is that boy?"

"Seven foot two inches, ma'am," he said.

She considered that for a few seconds, then shook her head and said, "I've never seen a nigger that tall."

I didn't react. I looked down into her wrinkled grand-motherly face and could tell that she had no idea that she was insulting me. To her, "nigger" was the same as saying "Negro," or "Afro-American," the polite term that was used back then. Confronting her would have been a waste of time.

But Coach Wooden did react. His whole body stiffened, his cheeks reddened. He looked at the old woman incredu-lously. He didn't know what to do, or how to respond. This was not his world. We had stepped out of his cocoon.

Mr. Sproatt was waving to another customer just arriv-ing. He had not heard the woman, or pretended not to have heard her. Coach looked up at me, clearly hoping I hadn't heard, either. But when he looked into my eyes, he knew I had.

Over the years, I often thought back to that moment and tried to see it from Coach's perspective. Did he wonder if I expected him to say something, to come to my defense as my coach, as an adult, as a white man? He had to be having a crisis of conscience: Go against his Midwestern morals by shouting at an old lady who wouldn't really understand his anger? Go against his Christian values by not standing up for a young boy who had been deeply insulted? Go against his patriotic values and not condemn her un-American racism?

In the end, he said nothing to her and she just walked away, never aware of the emotional chaos she had left in her doddering wake.

On the drive back to campus we both stared straight ahead at the road, unwilling to look each other in the eyes. Finally, he broke the uncomfortable silence: "You know, Lewis, sometimes you take people by surprise. Someone your size, it startles them."

"Uh-huh," I muttered, not sure where he was going with this.

More silence. He was carefully choosing each word. "Sometimes people will say things they don't mean or don't really understand. Please don't think all people are like that woman. Don't let ignorant people prompt an ignorant response from you. I know it's difficult, but let's not condemn everyone for the actions of a few."

Was he talking about her or himself? About what she said, or what he didn't say?

"Sure, Coach," I said. I didn't really want to talk about it. What was the point? There was nothing he could say that I hadn't heard before, mostly from well-meaning white people. I was used to it, so it was no big deal, but I could see it was eating him up. I didn't want that. I could see that he was a good man and that this incident was tearing him up inside.

We didn't talk about it again, but Coach never forgot that night. Interestingly, in describing that night when speaking publicly, he remembered it differently than I did. In his memory, the woman said, "Will you just look at that big black freak?" The word "nigger" was too painful even to store in his memory, and maybe it lessened his guilty feelings a little.

When he told a close friend, the great LSU coach Dale Brown, about this encounter, Coach Wooden said reflectively, "That really opened my eyes to things. I tried to become a lot more sensitive to stuff like that. My heart went out to Lewis. I thought, this is what he has to live with every day, and yes, my heart went out to him."

Nothing seemed to change between us after that night. He coached, I played. We didn't discuss race, he didn't ask me how I felt about what was happening, but there was a difference. We had gone to the restaurant to bond over steak and basketball and our intertwined futures, but we ended up being inexorably connected by what had happened in the parking lot. We had glimpsed into each other's hearts, and that had moved us beyond the coach–player relationship.

29

Reading Malcolm X: The Book That Changed My Life

I n the spring of 1966, I was almost nineteen and basking in being on an undefeated basketball team while maintaining a high grade point average. When basketball season was over, I was excited to have more time for reading. I had always been an avid reader, but now I was reading more intellectually challenging material. Most of what I read were assigned literary classics and textbooks, but I had also begun to read more political books on my own: Michael Harrington's *The Other America*, about poverty in the United States; Rachel Carson's *Silent Spring*, about environmental destruction from pesticides. But there was one book, published just a few months earlier, that I was especially compelled to read: *The Autobiography of Malcolm X*. Malcolm X, a fiery civil rights orator who had spoken aggressively against racism, had been assassinated a year earlier by three men from the Nation of Islam. They shot him twenty-one times.

I started the book with intellectual curiosity but soon began seeing the parallels between his life and mine. Our families were both from the Caribbean: His mother had come from Grenada, while my people came from nearby Trinidad. His father had been a follower of the black nationalist Marcus Garvey; my grandparents had been sympathetic to his ideas. His description of racism in his hometown of Lansing, Michigan, matched my experiences in New York and North Carolina. He pointed out that schoolroom textbooks ignored the role of black people, despite the fact that the first American martyr of the American Revolution was a black man named Crispus Attucks. My research at the Schomburg had revealed the same truths. Within a few pages, I was passionately engrossed, reading frantically yet not wanting the book to end.

In the popular young adult novel *The Fault in Our Stars*, John Green writes, "Sometimes, you read a book and it fills you with this weird evangelical zeal, and you become convinced that the shattered world will never be put back together unless and until all living humans read the book." That's how I felt when I finished the last page of Malcolm X and Alex Haley's book. I knew my life was changed forever, and I had to tell everyone I knew to *read this book now!* One passage particularly impressed me: "One day, I remember, a dirty glass of water was on a counter and Mr. Muhammad put a clean glass of water beside it. 'You want to know how to spread my teachings?' he said, and he pointed to the glasses of water. 'Don't condemn if you see a person has a dirty glass of water,' he said, 'just show them the clean glass of water that you have. When they inspect it, you won't have to say that yours is better.'" I was only nineteen years old, but I knew I'd been drinking from that dirty glass most of my life.

This was a time when most black Americans were holding their glasses of water up to the light and saying they were tired of waiting for white America to share the clean water.

I was riveted by Malcolm's intimate story of how he came to realize he'd been the victim of institutional racism, which had imprisoned him long before he'd landed in an actual prison. That's how I felt: imprisoned by an image of who I was supposed to be. The first thing Malcolm did was push aside the Baptist religion his parents had brought him up in and study Islam instead. To him, Christianity was a foundation of the white culture responsible for enslaving black people and a support for the racism that permeated society. His family had been attacked by the Christianity-spouting Ku Klux Klan and his home burned by a KKK splinter group, the Black Legion.

The Autobiography of Malcolm X starts as a political awakening, with Malcolm's angry polemic against white devils and a call to end racism "by any means necessary." His youthful anger and despair matched my own, and I found myself cheering him on as he helped spread the message of the Nation of Islam. But toward the end of the book, Malcolm begins to reject the hatred and violence that defined the Nation of Islam and embrace orthodox Sunni Islam. He traveled to Africa, made a pilgrimage to Mecca, and returned to preach about a world in which black and white people could come together.

Malcolm X's transformation from petty criminal to political leader to spiritual leader inspired me to look more closely at my own upbringing and forced me to think more deeply about my own identity. His explanation of how Islam helped him find his true self, and gave him the strength not only to face hostile reactions from both black and white critics but also to fight for social justice, led me to study the Quran. I knew that between 15 and 30 percent of African slaves had been Muslim, so exploring Islam was a way for me to connect with my African roots, which felt much more comfortable and authentic than Christianity, a religion that had historically devalued my ancestors.

The book was my own journey of political and spiritual awakening, and I emerged from it determined to find my political voice and spiritual calling. What's remarkable about *The Autobiography of Malcolm X* isn't how much it influenced me, but how many other people, black and white, experienced the same awakening as I did. Suburban white kids and urban black kids were all reading it.

The book didn't just shake *my* world—it shook *the* world.

In 1965, killers silenced the man, but not his voice. His words still live on today, as loud, as truthful, as hopeful as when he stood at a podium and addressed thousands. They certainly lived in me that day when I closed the last page of his book and started down a new path of religious exploration and political commitment.

30

Sophomore Year: Things Just Got Real

In some ways, my freshman year was like basic training, but my sophomore year was like being thrown into hand-to-hand combat. No matter how prepared you think you are, things go wrong.

The first step in my sophomore plan was to move out of the dorm and get an apartment. Teammate Edgar Lacey and I decided to get a place together. I'd saved up enough money from my $125-a-week summer job working in the New York offices of Columbia Pictures to buy a 1958 Mercedes and pay half the rent. First, we rented a small apartment in Santa Monica, but the rent proved too much of a strain, so we found a cheaper place in Pacific Palisades. Eventually, that also was unmanageable and we moved into the tinier maid's quarters in a condominium in Westwood.

We would practice to exhaustion every day, play games in front of thousands of cheering fans twice a week, and sacrifice our social life to balance academics and athletics, yet we never had any money.

"We should go to some other school," Edgar suggested as we sat in our tiny apartment.

"Where?" I asked.

"Anywhere we want, man! After last season, we could write our own ticket. You, me, and Lucius."

"The Three Black Musketeers," I said with a grin.

He laughed. "That's right. I'm the handsome one who gets all the girls."

"Aramis."

"Sure. Whatever." Then he sighed and shook his head. "I'm just saying, we could write our own ticket."

We weren't really serious about it, just griping as a way of bonding. Transferring to another school would have cost us a year of eligibility, and in reality, we would have faced the same financial restrictions. But none of the players, other than those who came from wealthy parents, were happy with our financial status. We knew the university was making a fortune off our efforts but wasn't willing to share any of it with us.

The other part of the sophomore plan was for the varsity team to win a national championship, especially after the disastrous last season. The pressure on Coach Wooden and the entire team was enormous, but the press had heaped a little more on me. The AP and UPI polls had ranked us as the number one team in the country. My face was suddenly on a bunch of national magazines, with *Sports Illustrated* showing me in a special foldout cover with an intimidating headline: "The New Superstar." Sure, I liked the attention, and most of the time I was confident that I could deliver on that promise. But sometimes I wanted to hide in the library and just read my books.

There would be no hiding. Every home game would be a sellout, and the school had scheduled as many home games as possible. When I walked by the Pauley Pavilion ticket office, students were lined up for two days before season tickets even went on sale. At night, they camped out in sleeping bags, and during the day, they did homework and threw Frisbees. UCLA had also made a deal with a local TV station to broadcast the games on tape delay, and Coach Wooden had agreed to do a weekly TV show discussing basketball. This was bigger—and more intimidating—than I could ever have imagined.

The team's plan for world dominance hit a snag when my roommate Edgar fractured his kneecap and needed surgery that would keep him off the court. He was an experienced upperclassman, and we needed his on-court expertise. Then Mike Lynn, another upperclassman with experience, pleaded guilty to credit card theft and was suspended for the season. Our starting lineup now included four sophomores and only one junior, Mike Warren. Suddenly, we were probably the least experienced team in the league.

Our best-laid plans had just been punched in the mouth.

If Coach Wooden felt the same pressure, he never let on. He showed up every day in his T-shirt, shorts, and athletic socks and shoes, a jacket with the word "Coach" on the back, and a whistle around his neck that seemed somehow louder and more accusatory than any whistle I'd ever heard before.

The biggest misconception people have about Coach Wooden is thinking that he focused on winning. It's an easy mistake to make because he was one of the winningest coaches in history. But he didn't. In fact, he did the opposite.

"Asking an athlete if he likes winning is like asking a Wall Street broker if he likes money," Coach told us in my freshman year. "Sure, we want to win. I love winning. But winning isn't our goal."

I didn't say anything, but clearly this was sports heresy. People have been burned at the stake for less.

One of the other freshman players raised his hand. "Coach Sanders says, 'Winning isn't everything; it's the only thing.'" He grinned a little, as if he'd just put one over on Coach.

Coach shook his head. Back in 1949, the UCLA football coach Henry Russell "Red" Sanders had uttered those immortal words after a loss to USC. Immediately, coaches everywhere had used it as a mantra to whip up their players into a winning frenzy.

"Winning is the by-product of hard work," Coach explained patiently, "like a pearl is the by-product of that clam fighting off a parasite."

"I thought it was a grain of sand," someone else said.

Coach ignored him. He didn't have time to educate us about science facts. "The goal is hard work. The reward is satisfaction that you pushed yourself to the edge physically, emotionally, and mentally. It is my firm belief that when everyone on a team works as hard as possible until they feel that glow of satisfaction in their hearts and peace of mind, that team is prepared for anything and anyone. Then winning is usually inevitable."

To a freshman, this was crazy talk. Was Coach having a stroke? Winning translated into attendance at games and alumni donations and television money; losing did not. His job and our scholarships depended on winning—that was a fiscal reality.

It took me years to fully appreciate this lesson. As a freshman, I admired Coach's sentiment even if I thought it was too esoteric. To me, you worked hard to beat your opponents. The satisfaction was in walking off the court with the fans screaming for your team, not theirs. But slowly, game by game, season by season, I started to see winning his way. Not just on the court, but off it as well.

But my sophomore year, my first time playing varsity, with all those magazines expecting great things from me, I wanted to win. I couldn't imagine the shame and embarrassment I would feel going back home having let my family, friends, and team down.

Most of our practices were team drills, but sometimes Coach Wooden worked just with me. I liked those private sessions because I knew I was learning something that would make me a better player. The two of us must have looked a little incongruous, with a five-foot-ten man standing on the sidelines next to his seven-foot-two center and demonstrating the fundamentals of rebounding. "Rebounding is positioning, Lewis," he emphasized. "If you are in the proper position, strength doesn't make a difference. All that contact around the basket is an effort to get the best position. Being quicker than your opponent to get that position negates his physical advantage." When he was teaching, he usually held a basketball in his hands and tried to look me in the eyes, or as close to my eyes as he could get. But somehow, when we did work on these things, the authority in his voice made him *sound* taller.

After we did our drills, we scrimmaged. During a game, what often appeared to be spontaneous on the court actually was the result of hours of practicing until our responses finally became automatic and instantaneous. We didn't have any set plays. We had a basic offensive system—you go here, you go there, you go in that corner, stand over there—and then we would run several options off it, depending on how our opponents defended us. Our offense was structured to recognize opportunities as a group and take advantage of them.

Coach emphasized teamwork over everything else. Teams

won games, not individuals. A good team had room for individuals to rise, but their rise had to lift everyone with them. That was the deal.

That's why Coach hated to see showboating during practice. He didn't even permit us to dunk. Practice was a work session; we ran, we drilled, we scrimmaged. We didn't experiment with showy moves. Willie Naulls, who started for UCLA in the mid-1950s and later influenced me to go there, told me how he had to learn to play within the Wooden system. After he made a couple of no-look passes, Wooden told him flatly, "No fancy stuff out there." His teammate Johnny Moore pulled Willie aside and warned him, "Two hands on the ball will get you some playing time. Don't do your no-lookers or you'll be on the bench watching me play." I took that advice to heart.

Wooden may not have liked anything fancy, but he was flexible enough to appreciate when an innovation truly worked. A lot of basketball fans don't know that the lob pass was created at UCLA by Larry Farmer and Greg Lee. I think if they had done it first in practice with Coach Wooden watching, they would not have done it a second time, but it happened spontaneously during a game. Larry Farmer raced down the sideline on a typical UCLA fast break, but this time, as the defense got set, he spun around his defender, and as he cut to the basket, Greg Lee, a world-class volleyball player, lobbed the ball over the top of the defense as if he were setting an outside hitter for a spike. Farmer caught the lob in midair and laid it into the basket. It evolved right out of the basic offense—it wasn't planned, it just presented itself.

Coach appreciated my hook shot, not just for its effectiveness in scoring but also for its finesse. We worked on it like two mechanics perfecting an engine. It was that hook that brought us together on the basketball court. Working on it gave us the opportunity to spend extended time in each other's presence. Both of us spoke fluent basketball, a language free of emotion. He loved that shot and saw in it possibilities I hadn't imagined. "It's an almost unstoppable shot," he told me. "If you can perfect it, it will enable you to dominate." Whatever furthered the artistry and aesthetic of basketball while increasing scoring potential, he liked.

Which is why he hated the slam dunk. He considered it nothing more than an arrogant display of brute force. The player leaps up and jams the ball through the hoop with enough force to rattle the whole backboard. To him, it was as primitive as urinating to mark one's territory. But to me, the dunk kicked up the adrenaline a notch, giving me an extra boost. After a dunk, I ran down the court with a little more energy.

We finished every practice by shooting free throws. We had to complete two in a row in order to leave. You had to stand on the line shooting until you made them. And then, just before we left, he would say, "Just remember, everything we've worked so hard to get done today can be destroyed if you make a bad choice between now and our next practice."

We understood what he meant by bad choices. No drugs or alcohol, no protesting in the streets. He wanted to protect his boys, but he was out of touch with how rapidly the culture was changing. The Beatles had arrived. Civil rights marches continued. Antiwar protests had begun. Women demanded rights most people didn't realize they had been denied. Rebellion was in the air. Nothing could stop it, even a well-meaning coach.

Our season opener was against our biggest rival, USC. Coach pulled me aside during practice to discuss his strategy.

"Lewis, this first game is very important to the rest of our season," he told me.

"Right, Coach," I said.

"So how should we handle this?"

Was he asking me? *I just work here,* I wanted to say. But he waited for me to answer. His patience was unnerving.

"Wellll," I said, stretching the word as I thought. "I would go at them as hard as possible, score as many points as possible, and let them and everyone else in the league know we mean business." I'd said it all in one breath.

Coach Wooden smiled up at me. "Then let's do that."

And that's exactly what we did. We beat them 105–90. I scored fifty-six points, a new school record by fourteen points. "At times, he frightens me," Coach told the press after the game. "When he gets it all together, he's going to be something."

That game did indeed announce to the world who we were and what we could do. We finished the season 30–0, reclaiming the NCAA National Basketball Championship for Coach Wooden and UCLA.

31

The Cleveland Summit Changes the Way the World Sees Me

After our tremendous sophomore season, I was even more famous. The articles about me were no longer about my great potential, but about how that potential had been realized. The coach of the New York Knicks was saying, "Alcindor could play for any pro team right now." Coach Wooden tried to downplay the press coverage to relieve the pressure it put on me. "Lew has improved," he told reporters, "but he still has a long way to go to attain the maturity and experience he needs." He was right, and I was grateful to him for telling them so.

Coach had tried to warn me about the relentless press that evening at the Bat Rack, before we'd gotten sidetracked by the little old lady at the front door calling me a nigger. There was a lot of praise for my play, yes, but articles had started to speculate about me personally. Why didn't I smile more? What personal problems was I hiding? The truth was pretty boring: I was just shy. Having my photo taken made me uncomfortable; talking about myself all the time to endless reporters embarrassed me. I loved playing, but afterward I just wanted to read a book or sit quietly in a jazz club with a couple of friends.

I felt disconcerted about my fame because I didn't yet know what to do with it. I had a lot of political opinions, and now I had a national platform. But I didn't want to just ramble on about injustice; I wouldn't be taken seriously. I would be dismissed as just another whining college kid.

That changed in May when football great Jim Brown, who had become a Hollywood actor, invited me to join a group of black athletes and activists in Cleveland to discuss Muhammad Ali's refusal to be drafted. At twenty, I would be the youngest person at what would become known as the Cleveland Summit. The meeting was to determine whether we would publicly support Ali in his refusal to be drafted.

This was by no means a rubber-stamp committee. Several of the participants had been in the military. Brown himself had belonged to the army ROTC and graduated from Syracuse University as a second lieutenant. Carl Stokes, an attorney who in a few months would become the mayor of Cleveland, making him the first black mayor of a major US city, had served in World War II, just like Coach Wooden.

The summit was not even supposed to happen. It had started as a simple phone call to Brown from Ali's manager, Herbert Muhammad. Muhammad wanted Brown to help persuade Ali to drop his refusal to be drafted, to avoid the severe loss of income that could financially wipe Ali out, not to mention the public outcry. Muhammad was torn between his religious convictions, which were the same as Ali's, and his desire to protect his friend from ruin. Ali was only twenty-five, so two years in the army wouldn't drastically affect his boxing career. To Muhammad, Brown seemed like a good choice to convince Ali because he had been an outspoken activist for years, so Ali would listen. But Brown also was a partner in the company that promoted Ali's fights, so he had a financial stake in having Ali keep fighting.

Brown took his role seriously. He invited me and the rest of the summit members to sit as a jury in assessing Ali's sin-

cerity and commitment. Every athlete responded by immediately agreeing to come at his own expense. I was excited
to finally be part of the political movement in a more direct
and active way. I also wanted to help Ali if I could because
he made me feel proud to be African American.

On June 4, 1967, we gathered in the offices of the Negro
Industrial and Economic Union, which soon became the
Black Economic Union. Despite our admiration for Ali, we
grilled him for hours. Many on the group had come with
their minds already made up to persuade Ali to accept his
military service. The discussions became pretty heated
as questions and answers were fired back and forth. Pretty
soon, though, we all realized Ali was not going to change
his mind. For two hours, he lectured us on Islam and black
pride and his religious conviction that the Vietnam War was
wrong.

We were all well aware that in the early days of the
Vietnam War, kids who could afford to go to college were
exempted from the draft, which left poor kids, many of them
black, forced to go fight. Ali argued that it was a war against
people of color fought by people of color for a country that
denied them their basic civil rights.

In the end, he convinced us and we decided to support

him. Bill Russell summed it up for all of us by saying, "I envy Muhammad Ali....He has something I have never been able to attain, and something very few people possess: He has absolute and sincere faith. I'm not worried about Muhammad Ali. He is better equipped than anyone I know to withstand the trials in store for him. What I'm worried about is the rest of us."

We did our best at that Cleveland Summit to support Ali's legal fight and to publicize the injustice of the draft, but we knew how powerless we were against those promoting the war. Nevertheless, I was thrilled that I was finally doing something important rather than just complaining.

Being at that summit and hearing Ali's articulate defense of his moral beliefs and his willingness to suffer for them reinvigorated my own commitment to become even more politically involved.

Coach Wooden, however, was not a fan of Muhammad Ali.

After the bombing of Pearl Harbor, John Wooden left his wife, son, and daughter, and his career as a high school English teacher, coach, and professional basketball player, to join the US Navy. He served as a physical education instructor for four years during World War II. When a sudden attack of appendicitis prevented Lieutenant Wooden from shipping out with his buddies for the South Pacific on the USS *Franklin*, he was quickly replaced by a friend and fraternity brother, Purdue quarterback Freddie Stalcup. The *Franklin* was soon attacked by a Japanese kamikaze plane that crashed into the ship, killing Stalcup. The loss of his friend, as well as the knowledge that it could have been he who died, made Coach cherish the sacrifices of soldiers. It also made him less tolerant of those who shirked their military duty.

While I was at UCLA, Coach and I never had an extended conversation about Ali, but he would drop comments critical of the boxer now and then. He knew that Ali and I were friends, so his remarks were always in passing. "First he's Cassius Clay, then he's Muhammad Ali. Hmph." "It's a privilege, not an obligation, to fight for your country." "Can't he see he's hurting the country?"

I ignored these comments. I felt like the child of divorced parents who had to listen to one beloved parent complain about the other beloved parent. I respected and admired both of them, and I wanted to maintain my relationship with both. Despite my growing political activism, I still loved basketball. It was an island of refuge for me. I knew the rules, I had the skills, and the outcome was always clean and pure.

With politics, there never seemed to be a resolution, just more obstacles.

Ali was an irritant between us, but not a relationship breaker. I respected Coach's position as a veteran, but I knew Ali was on the right path, a path that Coach couldn't understand. He was too loyal to old ideas. To me, he was like the US Constitution: The original had some flaws (like not providing rights for women and permitting slavery), but it also had provisions to evolve with the times, to grow in order to fulfill the spirit of equality that defined the document—this defined Coach's personal philosophy. Coach was never static in his beliefs, but rather he evolved over the years as he read and observed more. By 2009, he told an interviewer that he would describe himself politically as a liberal Democrat who had voted for some Republican presidential candidates.

He even came to respect Muhammad Ali. In 2007, when Coach was ninety-seven years old, he visited the Muhammad Ali Center in Louisville, Kentucky. When he returned to Los Angeles, we got together for breakfast at his favorite restaurant, VIP's, and he pummeled me with questions about Ali. What is he like? How bad was his Parkinson's? Did I see him at all? Ali used to come to some of my games when I was with the Lakers, and I would go to some of his boxing matches. We still stayed in touch, but his health kept him from traveling much. I could see the respect for Ali in Coach's face.

The Cleveland Summit had catapulted me from grumbling college sophomore to a national spokesperson for political and social issues involving African Americans. It was what I had wanted, but the pressure was even greater than it was playing basketball because the stakes were so much higher. Winning a basketball game wasn't the same as trying to secure voting rights, educational opportunities, and jobs for the disenfranchised. Failing to score on a hook shot meant missing a couple of points. Failing to articulate a position clearly and convincingly could affect people's lives.

It was scary, but I felt ready. As Malcolm X had said, "If you want something, you had better make some noise."

32

Junior Year: Great Expectations, Great Disappointments

I spent that summer working for the New York City Housing Authority, giving basketball clinics around the city to young black kids. I was excited to teach them basketball skills, but I was just as excited to instill in them a sense of black pride. It is difficult for young people today to understand that in the 1960s, black pride was an important issue because black kids didn't see themselves as being as valuable as white kids. How could they when they saw segregation being tolerated, even though it was against federal laws? And they knew they would have to work twice as hard to get into schools white kids would be easily accepted into. I was happy to be doing more than talking about injustice, but actually making a difference with young black kids.

I returned to UCLA ready to play basketball, but one important thing had changed: The NCAA had outlawed the dunk, declaring it was "not a skillful shot." That ruling, which most people referred to as the Lew Alcindor Rule, came as no surprise to Coach Wooden. In fact, initially he was concerned the NCAA actually was going to take more extreme steps to curtail UCLA's dominance of the game. And by UCLA, he meant Lew Alcindor. Although I didn't know this at the time, he was fearful the NCAA might raise the height of the basket or, in a more extreme action, ban me from the game.

At the time of the ruling, I was pretty upset. It felt as if the entire NCAA had gotten together just to punish me for scoring too many points. It was hard not to take that personally. Coach Wooden said publicly that it had been adopted after Houston players bent the rim dunking during pregame warm-ups in the 1967 NCAA Tournament, but no one believed that. Whatever the explanation, the reality was that dunking was no longer a part of my arsenal.

As usual, Coach Wooden took the most optimistic

approach, telling me, "It doesn't make any difference whether you are the reason or not. It's going to make you a better basketball player. You're just going to have to further develop the rest of your game."

"Like what?" I asked angrily.

"Like your flat hook. There's room for improvement there, Lewis."

"Sure, but what will keep them from banning that, too?"

Coach sighed. "You have an obstacle, Lewis. What you do about that obstacle defines who you are."

So we worked on my hook. His persistence in the face of my petulance built a closer relationship between us. I came to the realization that he wouldn't give up on me. I knew he wanted me to perfect the hook so I could be more effective in the games, but there was something in his attitude, a patient understanding, that made me feel he was more interested in teaching me how to adapt to disappointment. To push through. To endure.

Coach taught me the techniques to hone the hook into my iconic shot that carried me through championships in college and the pros. But his real lesson about perseverance and adaption has carried me through life beyond the basketball court.

The NCAA removed the dunking ban in 1976, but by then I had been playing pro ball for several years. Twelve years after the dunk was reinstated, toward the end of my professional career, Coach Wooden admitted to me that *he had been among those who had voted to ban the dunk.*

I knew Coach's integrity too well by then to feel even a hint of betrayal. Even so, I couldn't help but ask him about it.

"Coach, why would you vote to ban the dunk?"

He didn't hesitate. "I thought it was for the good of the game."

"Whose game? It hurt UCLA more than any other team."

He hesitated, then sighed. "It's an ugly shot, Kareem. Nothing but brute force."

That stung a little. I wasn't known for my brute force.

"The game is about teamwork," he added. "The dunk is about embarrassing your opponent."

"Sometimes," I said. "But sometimes it's about timing and grace. Two skills you taught me."

"Flattery won't work," he said, grinning.

We never did agree on that issue. But by then, Coach and I had been friends for many years, and we knew that friends don't have to agree in order to respect each other's opinions. Coach had earned my respect long ago, not just for his coaching ability in leading us to win, but for his poise when we lost. It's easy to be gracious and magnanimous when you're winning, but he taught us that it takes character to be those things when you lose. Especially when the game is an important one. And they didn't come any more important than our January 20, 1968, game against the University of Houston Cougars—a matchup that everyone called "the Game of the Century."

It was the first NCAA regular season game to be shown nationwide on prime-time television. We had played the Cougars the previous season in the semifinals of the NCAA Tournament and crushed them 73–58, going on to win the tournament. After the game, Elvin Hayes, the Cougars' best player, had challenged me in the press by saying I hadn't played tough defense, hadn't been aggressive rebounding, and wasn't as good a player as I was hyped to be.

"Oh, man," my roommate, Edgar, said after I read it aloud. "Hayes let you have it good."

"You *were* a little lazy on defense," Lucius teased.

Edgar nodded. "And you could've snagged a few more rebounds. Just saying."

I laughed. "I appreciate the support."

I may have laughed it off with my teammates, but I really wanted to take Houston down again, especially in front of the first nationwide TV audience.

Because of our forty-seven-game winning streak, we were heavily favored, but a week before the game, the cornea of my left eye was scratched in a game, which left me in a hospital bed for three days with a patch over my eye. I missed two games, which my teammates won handily without me. However, during my recovery, I was not allowed to move, which meant no practicing or conditioning before the Houston game. Plus, my eyesight was severely restricted.

This was an obstacle, but as Coach had said when they banned dunking, "What you do about that obstacle defines who you are."

We walked down the ramp of the Houston Astrodome to fifty-three thousand cheering fans, twice the previous record of people to watch a live basketball game. The excitement from the crowd was overwhelming.

Unfortunately, being emotionally moved didn't fix my eye or my lack of conditioning. I played the worst game of my UCLA career. My teammates picked up the slack and kept the game competitive. The crowd was yelling so loudly that we couldn't hear the ball when we dribbled. We were tied right up until the final seconds, when a foul sent Elvin Hayes to the foul line. He sank both shots. We lost 71–69.

I scored only fifteen points and shot less than 50 percent. Worse, it looked to everyone else as if Elvin Hayes was right about me. The team was devastated. We were humiliated on TV in front of millions of fans. But Coach sauntered into the locker room, shrugged, and said, "Tonight they were the better team."

No excuses, no blame. No running down the other team.

I felt a mixture of resentfulness and envy for him. My stomach was churning inside as if I'd swallowed a barracuda and it was gnawing everything in sight. Coach looked fresh and chipper and ready to go another round. I wished I felt that way. He was going home and would undoubtedly fall into a restful sleep. I would lie in bed staring at the ceiling, reliving every play, every point, every missed shot.

Fortunately, we had another shot at redemption. Neither the Cougars nor our team lost another game the rest of the season, which led us to a rematch in the NCAA Men's Division I Tournament semifinals. Despite Coach Wooden's Zen approach to our loss to Houston, I was still a college kid with a drive to win. After beating us, Elvin Hayes had continued to berate me in the press. That same week, *Sports Illustrated*'s cover featured a photo of Elvin scoring over me. I tore the cover off and pasted it on my locker to remind me to practice harder, longer, and with more intensity.

This time we destroyed them, 101–69. We were jubilant in the locker room, celebrating our revenge. After the game, I did something I had never done before: I put on a bright red, orange, and yellow African robe called a dashiki, which I referred to as my "dignity robe." My joy that night was more powerful than my reticence. It wasn't meant to be a challenge to anyone; it simply was my statement that I was finding my roots. And I wasn't ashamed to express them.

Coach Wooden, who had been talking with a reporter, turned at the sound of my dashiki swishing and saw me in all my brightly colored finery. He hesitated while he took it all in, then smiled broadly like a father watching his son in a school play.

Then he gathered us together, his expression the same as it had been when we'd lost. He congratulated us for a game well played. He made sure we acknowledged Coach Norman, whose diamond-and-one defense helped us contain the Cougars' top scorer, Elvin Hayes, who had been averaging 37.7 points a game but that night scored only 10.

Coach walked out of the room, and I knew he was going home to his wife and another restful sleep. I would be up celebrating in my bright African robe—and later lying in bed, reliving every play, every point, every missed shot.

We finished the season winning another NCAA National Championship. But it was that single loss, and our ability to come back from it even stronger, that most defined us.

33

Bruce Lee Becomes My Teacher

I met Bruce Lee in 1967, the fall semester of my junior year at UCLA. He was not yet the international superstar he would soon become. He was just a struggling actor teaching martial arts to pay the rent and support his wife and baby boy.

I'd been training in aikido during the summer back home in New York City. I got the idea of taking up martial arts the previous year when I saw one of the Zatoichi samurai movies at the Kokusai Theater on Crenshaw Boulevard near campus. After watching the balletic movements of Zatoichi as he gracefully evaded violent gangs of opponents and left them all helpless, I figured learning that kind of body control could only help me in games when I was being double- and triple-teamed. Instead of brute force, I would slide and roll and slip by them without fouling. After only a couple of months, I quickly found my senses were sharper and my reflexes quicker.

When I returned to UCLA for the fall semester, I knew I wanted to continue my training so I asked a friend of mine who ran *Black Belt* magazine where I should go in Los Angeles. He told me about this young guy out in Culver City, the west side of Los Angeles, who had played the martial arts sidekick Kato on the single season of the TV series *The Green Hornet*. I was a little skeptical of training with a television actor, but my friend assured me that this man was the real deal. He had already built a reputation as something of a maverick in the martial arts community, with his own unorthodox ideas of combat, but his skills were widely acclaimed to be remarkable. He was known for demonstrating the one-inch punch—a punch from only one inch away from the target that generated enough force to break boards or knock an opponent to the floor.

Bruce was the kind of person who could win you over within twenty seconds of meeting him. Most martial arts instructors I had met before were very stiff and formal, constantly demanding overt demonstrations of respect. Not Bruce. He greeted me with a broad smile and friendly demeanor, and right away I knew this was not a scowling teacher from Japanese films demanding bowing obedience. We talked UCLA basketball for a while and then got down to business.

Bruce asked his wife, Linda, to assist him in a demonstration. He told me to brace myself behind the heavy punching bag that hung by a chain from the ceiling. The bag was as thick and heavy as a body. "Hold it as tight as you can," he instructed me.

Bruce told Linda to kick the bag.

"Bruce, I don't think this will work," I said. "I'm two feet taller and a hundred pounds heavier than Linda."

Bruce smiled but said nothing.

"Just hold the bag tight, Lew," Linda said.

I squatted behind the bag and hugged it tightly. I was confident that even a truck wouldn't be able to budge it.

"Ready?" Bruce said.

"Ready," I said, a little smugly.

Bruce nodded at Linda.

Suddenly Linda fired off a kick straight into the bag. The impact rocked me backward a few feet, readjusted my spine, and possibly rearranged the order of my teeth.

They stood there smiling at the shocked expression on my face.

"Okay," I said, rubbing my chest. "Teach me that."

Bruce's approach was similar to that of Coach Wooden. They both emphasized practicing fundamentals over and over. Bruce used to say, "I fear not the man who has practiced ten thousand kicks once, but I fear the man who has practiced one kick ten thousand times." For me, my hook shot was the one kick practiced ten thousand times.

Both also emphasized preparation. The winning athlete prepared for competition by training the body and the mind to anticipate all contingencies. While Coach Wooden told us, "Failing to prepare is preparing to fail," Bruce would say, "Preparation for tomorrow is hard work today." The seventeenth-century swordsman Miyamoto Musashi, author of *The Book of Five Rings*, which Bruce and I often discussed at great length, wrote, "You can only fight the way you practice." The message from all three coaches was the same, and I took it to heart. I dedicated myself to preparation by maintaining complete focus during basketball practice and my training with Bruce. As a result, I became stronger, faster, and a much more intense player.

Bruce's most significant teaching was that when it came

to martial arts, there was no single technique or philosophy that was the correct way. This was very different from other teachers who each seemed to belong to a single school of teaching. This was how Bruce developed his Jeet Kune Do (Way of the Intercepting Fist) method: Each fighter is unique, as is each fight. Therefore, the fighter must constantly adapt, using multiple techniques and approaches. This was also a belief Coach Wooden had. Both wanted their pupils to reach a level where they could teach themselves how to continue to improve.

Bruce was—to me, to his friends, and to himself—first and foremost a philosopher. Although it was his almost supernatural physical abilities that attracted his students, including movie stars, it was his equally remarkable intellectual abilities that kept us coming back. He had taken philosophy and psychology classes in college and was eager to discuss the principles he'd learned. Bruce and I spent as much time talking about books as we did sparring on the mat.

Bruce and I had something else in common: We both had experienced brutal discrimination. Bruce came from an acting family and had been performing onstage and in Chinese films since he was a child. When he came to the United States from Hong Kong as a teenager, he briefly abandoned acting to teach martial arts. Eventually, he did return to acting, and he was driven to share his philosophy of martial arts with the world through his acting. But Hollywood saw him only as an Asian, and the only acting parts for Asians were villains or servants. His frustration with Hollywood prompted him to return to Hong Kong to make movies.

In Hong Kong, he started making martial arts films like *Fist of Fury* and *The Big Boss*, which became huge international hits. Finally, he had the fame and success that had been denied him in America. And kids all around the world were flocking to martial arts studios to learn Bruce's Jeet Kune Do.

In July 1973, I was twenty-six years old and spending my summer break from the Milwaukee Bucks letting my nerd flag fly by traveling throughout the Middle East learning Arabic. On my way home, I decided to stop off in Hong Kong to visit Bruce. We had recently done a movie together called *Game of Death*, in which I played someone wearing awesome sunglasses who gets killed by Bruce. I think my sunglasses turned in a better performance than I did, but Bruce was his usual dynamic, funny, and cocky on-screen persona that the world so loved to watch. And we had great fun shooting that scene together.

When I landed at the Singapore airport, I saw the headlines that Bruce had died. I was stunned, of course, and saddened that I had lost such a good friend. But I was also aware of how profoundly his death would affect the rest of the world. He was only thirty-two when he died, but he had already revolutionized the way the world saw martial arts, both as a form of entertainment in movies and on TV and, more important, as a philosophy and way of life.

Despite having had many ups and downs in his life, despite having been poor and rich, despite being snubbed and internationally acclaimed, he lived by a simple guiding principle: "Think lightly of yourself and deeply of the world."

I was twenty when I met Bruce Lee, but his teachings, both in his studio and by his example, have stayed with me the rest of my life.

34

Why I Didn't Play in the 1968 Olympics

n 1960, an eighteen-year-old Cassius Clay walked into a Louisville, Kentucky, restaurant wearing the Olympic gold medal in boxing he had just won for the glory of the United States. He was aware that restaurants in his hometown were segregated, but he was so optimistic after winning the gold medal that he thought the world had changed. "Man, I know I'm going to get my people freedom now," he later recalled thinking. "I'm the champion of the whole world, the Olympic champion. I know I can eat downtown now." But when he sat down, he was refused service and told to leave. "I had to leave that restaurant, in my hometown, where I went to church and served in their Christianity, and fought—my daddy fought in all the wars. Just won the gold medal and couldn't eat downtown. I said, 'Something's wrong.'"

In 1968, I was asked to join the men's basketball Olympic team. I was twenty-one years old and well aware that whatever choice I made would send a message to black and white Americans. I was torn. Joining the team would signal that I supported the way people of color were being treated in America—which I didn't. Not joining the team could look like I didn't love America—which I did.

Complicating my thinking was that Dr. Martin Luther King Jr., the cheerful, optimistic man, had just been assassinated by a white man with a rifle.

Three of my heroes—civil rights activist Medgar Evers, Malcolm X, and Martin Luther King Jr.—had all been assassinated within five years. Two months after Dr. King was shot, Robert F. Kennedy, who was running for president with promises to advance the cause of civil rights, was also gunned down. It seemed that anybody who spoke publicly in favor of civil rights was a target for assassination.

What is difficult for many white people to understand is the extent to which black people go through each day fearing for their lives. In the 1960s, white people could get away with discriminating against black citizens in jobs, housing,

and education without much fear of government interven-
tion. Because the government wasn't doing that much to
prevent it, racists felt emboldened to act out their hostili-
ties by committing violent acts against black people. Racists
often take their cues on how to act from the way the government behaves. If the government is actively campaigning
against racism, they hide their feelings and do nothing. If the
government is indifferent to racism by not prosecuting it,
then they feel it's okay to come out of hiding and attack.

In 1968, we felt under attack, and we couldn't go to the
authorities because they were the ones attacking. That year,
there were riots in more than one hundred cities across the
country, and the image many people saw on their televisions every night was of police beating black protesters and
students.

Whatever Coach Wooden's political beliefs were when I
played for him, he never openly judged my beliefs. In April
1968, just after Dr. King had been assassinated, I joined in
a silent campus demonstration in support of his political
agenda. This was as laid-back as a protest rally could get:
a bunch of students ambling around Bruin Walk carrying
signs for an hour. We were so polite and unaggressive, we
could have been gathering for a tie-dye demonstration. Still,

we enraged some people who felt compelled to ask me what I was doing. "You're going to play in the NBA some day and make millions! Why aren't you more grateful? This country gave you everything! You're gonna be richer than most white people!" I tried to be patient and explain that my own success had nothing to do with the issues, but they didn't want to hear it.

Coach Wooden knew all about my participation at the protest, but he never said a word to me. No dirty looks. No biting comments in passing. He acted as if he didn't know about it, which I chose to take as approval. Not that I needed his approval. I was already committed to becoming more openly active.

A few months earlier, the sociology professor Harry Edwards had gathered together a group of black athletes who had been invited to compete in the Olympics to discuss the possibility of boycotting it.

"Why should I bring home a medal for a country that won't make sure I can vote?" asked one angry athlete.

"Look, man, you're right," said another, "but I may never get this chance again. I've been training my whole life to compete in the Olympics. I deserve my shot."

"Maybe we can do both," suggested another athlete. "If

we win a medal, we can make some speech about racism at home."

"They'll take away your medal and kick you out."

"Yeah," he said, "but at least I'll have won it."

And so the discussion went. At the end, we couldn't all agree to boycott, but I decided I would not go. I felt my presence would be an endorsement that everything was okay. Instead, I returned to my summer job from the previous year, teaching kids in New York City how to play basketball and why they should stay in school. My decision not to play resulted in hate mail calling me, among other things, "an ungrateful nigger."

Among our boycott discussion group were the runners Tommie Smith and John Carlos, who decided to travel to Mexico City to compete in the Olympics. They won the gold and bronze medals in the two-hundred-meter sprint, but when they stood on the platform after receiving their medals, they raised their black-gloved fists over their heads in what was then called the "Black Power Salute." They wore black gloves showing unity with all African Americans, black socks with no shoes to symbolize high poverty rates among black people, and a scarf (Smith) and beads (Carlos) to symbolize the history of lynchings. They were immediately suspended and kicked out. They returned to the United States as heroes to many African Americans—myself included—and rabble-rousers to many white people. They received numerous death threats. But their gesture sparked a national discussion of racism in the United States.

That summer ended with the Democratic National Convention in Chicago, three days in August that were so violent, so contentious, and so chaotic that books, movies, and even songs have been written about it. While Democrats inside the convention were choosing their nominee to run for president against the Republican former vice president, Richard Nixon, outside there were ten thousand protesters, mostly students, being beaten by twenty-three thousand police and National Guardsmen. So much tear gas was dispersed that it wafted throughout the city. The Walker Report, a study issued later by the panel established to investigate the incident, described it as "unrestrained and indiscriminate police violence . . . made all the more shocking by the fact that it was often inflicted upon persons who had broken no law, disobeyed no order, made no threat."

This was what was going on in the country in the summer months before my senior year at UCLA. Their voices were speaking out against injustice, and they were being silenced by violence.

Given all this, going to Mexico to win medals didn't seem to be the highest priority for me. What became a priority, as it had been since I'd participated in the Cleveland Summit, was adding my voice to those who were trying to explain why black Americans were in such pain. Watching Smith and Carlos on TV with their fists raised defiantly, I realized that even though I was only twenty-one, I still had to speak up. Sometimes it felt as if we were at the bottom of a well, shouting up to a crowd of people dressed in white summer clothes and having a garden party. Their laughter and conversation and music drowned out our cries for help, so we had no choice but to shout louder and louder, hoping someone would hear us.

35

Why I Converted to Islam

That summer, while I was wrestling with forming my political beliefs, I was also examining my spiritual beliefs. The biggest challenge of growing up is sifting through all the unasked-for influences that push and pull you in different directions and deciding for yourself which ones you will follow. Like every other kid, I had many influences: what my parents wanted, what my teachers wanted, what my religion wanted, what society wanted, what my peers wanted, and what my coaches wanted. There were so many that I had to examine each one to figure out which ones were what *I* wanted.

I had already decided on my political beliefs by publicly supporting Muhammad Ali and by publicly boycotting the

Olympics. And that summer I also decided on my spiritual beliefs by converting to Islam.

I had been interested in various religions since arriving at UCLA and deciding to abandon my Catholic upbringing. I still had a deep desire to understand what God meant to me and how that understanding would affect my actions. I read extensively about Buddhism, Taoism, existentialism, and various Protestant beliefs. I kept an open mind about each as I also delved into the godless void of Friedrich Nietzsche and the multi-god universe of Hinduism. I didn't really connect fully with any of them. All I knew was that I wasn't an atheist—I believed there was a God, and that God wanted us to do good.

"Man, just pick one," my friend Jimmy Johnson said, pointing at the stack of religious books on my desk.

"I will," I said. "When I'm ready."

"Opium of the people. That's what Karl Marx called religion. Makes 'em all sheep."

"People just want to do the right thing," I said. "This helps them."

"If they all just want to do the right thing, then what's the difference which one you pick?"

Good question. I wasn't looking for just a set of heavenly

ordained rules, I was looking for a religion that I identified with culturally as well as spiritually. Which is why I chose Islam.

My interest in Islam began while reading *The Autobiography of Malcolm X*. The religion gave him strength to completely transform himself from illiterate street hoodlum to articulate spokesperson for hundreds of thousands of black Americans. I started to read many books about Islam because of his inspiration, but my continuing interest was based on my own needs and observations. I was looking to connect not just with the religious teachings but with the heritage of the people who followed Islam. I knew there were a billion or more Muslims divided mostly among the two largest sects: Sunni Islam and the far smaller Shia Islam. I knew most Muslims lived in Central and South Asia, the Middle East, and North Africa. I knew that many of the slaves brought from Africa were Muslims.

I knew enough to know I wanted to learn more. So instead of going to the Olympics in Mexico City that summer, I began attending a Sunnite mosque on 125th Street.

I'm often asked why I picked a religion so foreign to American culture. Some fans took it very personally, as if I'd firebombed their church while tearing up an American flag.

Actually, I was rejecting the religion that was foreign to *my* black African culture and embracing one that was part of my racial heritage. Fans also thought I had joined the Nation of Islam, the American Islamic movement founded in Detroit in 1930. I didn't join them; I rejected them emphatically. Instead, I studied the Sunni sect of Islam.

My parents were not pleased by my conversion. Though they weren't strict Catholics, they had raised me to believe in Christianity as gospel. But the more I studied history, especially of the church, the more disillusioned I became with the role of Christianity in subjugating my people. I knew, of course, that the Second Vatican Council in 1965 had declared slavery to be an "infamy" that dishonored God and was a poison to society, but for me, it was too little, too late. They came to that conclusion a hundred years after the Emancipation Proclamation! The failure of the church to use its might and influence to stop slavery made me angry. And while I realize that many Christians risked their lives and families to fight against slavery, and that it would not have been ended without them, I found it hard to align myself with the cultural institutions that had turned a blind eye to such outrageous behavior in direct violation of their most sacred beliefs. I also knew that the slave owner named Alcindor who owned my ancestors was Christian.

That summer before my senior year, I walked into the mosque wearing my bright African robe that I had worn only once before, after defeating Houston in the semifinals. Everyone else was wearing white. My big show of cultural unity was a major fail. I felt like the teenage nerd in a movie who shows up at a party wearing a clown outfit because he'd been told it was a dress-up party, but everyone else is in tuxedos and formal gowns.

One man approached me and asked politely, "Are you looking for the African Cultural Center? It's downstairs."

"No," I told him, "this is the right place. I'm here to worship."

He handed me a prayer booklet that contained several chapters from the Quran translated from Arabic. "You must memorize them," he instructed.

I took the booklet home and memorized the chapters. I learned that memorizing a couple of the 114 suras (chapters) of the Quran is a goal of many adherents, and that millions have done so. I realized that this was the spiritual equivalent of my "muscle memory" training from both Coach Wooden and Bruce Lee. The athletic world encourages repeating a movement until the body reacts without hesitation; the spiritual encourages repeating the 6,236 verses of the Quran until you do good without hesitation.

I returned to the mosque when possible, immersing myself into the people and the religion. Each visit reenergized me as if at last I had found my place, my people, and my path. Finally, one Friday, before witnesses, I pronounced my *shahada*, which is the proclamation: "There is no god but Allah. Muhammad is the messenger of Allah." I was a Muslim. As such, I was given a new name by my teacher: Abdul ("servant of Allah") Kareem ("generous"). I kept the name secret from everyone but my closest friends and my parents. Everyone still called me Lew.

My reluctance to proclaim my new name wasn't just shyness or the need for privacy. Part of me recognized a contradiction. I was on a spiritual quest to define who I was and what I believed in—to forge my own identity. I had chosen my political positions. And I had chosen my religion. But in neither case had I chosen my name. My parents named me Lew, and a slave owner in Haiti indirectly named me Alcindor. Now my Muslim teacher named me. I was still too naive and too new to the religion to argue about my name, but I knew that my journey of growing up was still not quite over.

Which is why I was relieved to find a new coach, Hamaas Abdul-Khaalis, who would shepherd me through the intricacies of becoming a more devout Muslim.

Hamaas was born Ernest McGee. He had been a drummer and knew my father from their days running in the same musician circles. Here was yet another man who had changed his name on the path to becoming the person he wanted to be. I had started to understand that all these name changers were following the example of the very first immigrants who founded America. They had come here to reinvent themselves according to their own beliefs rather than someone else's. Now I was a part of that sacred American tradition.

After my first meeting with Hamaas, who was very learned about Islam, it became clear just how ignorant I was and how much I had to learn. He agreed to mentor me, so for the rest of the summer I got up every morning at four thirty in order to be at his house by six o'clock. Then I'd hurry off to my job by nine. He instructed me on every aspect of Islam. He had very strict ideas about everything Islam demanded from true Muslims, and there was no bending these rules. He also knew of my political disenchantment with the United States, having heard me state with youthful arrogance that though I lived here, America wasn't really my country.

"Don't ever say that this isn't your country," he instructed me very firmly. "Your ancestors lived and died in this country and this is your country. You have to get all your rights as a citizen. Don't reject it, affirm it."

I was stunned. If anyone knew the horrors this country had put black people through, it would be him. I had expected him to be on my side. But the more I studied with him, the more I understood that rather than sit around complaining about what the country wasn't doing, he wanted us to work hard to help the country do what it should be doing. He talked about the many white Americans who wanted to make things better for everyone and suffered personal sacrifices to make it happen. We owed it to them to show compassion and kindness. That was the Muslim way; that was the American way.

That summer, Hamaas's teachings about Islam brought me closer to being an American.

At the end of the summer, I once again pronounced my *shahada*, this time before Hamaas. I shaved my head and shared a ceremonial meal, *akikat*, with the community. Hamaas then decided I needed to be renamed; Abdul Kareem wasn't enough. Kareem means "noble" and "generous"; Abdul means "servant." "But we're missing your spirit." He smiled. "Jabbar. That means 'powerful.'"

Now I was Kareem Abdul-Jabbar. I was happy with my religion, with my teacher, with my community, with my name. But deep down, I knew something was missing. I just couldn't identify it.

36

Senior Year: One and Done

When I returned to UCLA for my final year, everything on the outside was the same as ever. Classes. Friends. Practice. Travel. But I was not the same. I felt as if I had outgrown the quaint limits of the campus and already had my eyes on life after college. My political interests in black culture and my studies in Islam isolated me from most of the other students. Even my enthusiasm for basketball had lessened somewhat. We had lost only one game in three years, so there wasn't a lot to prove anymore.

I hadn't spoken about my religious conversion with anyone on the team. I wasn't being mysterious or secretive; I just didn't know how to bring it up. "Hey, fellas, let's go out tonight and crush those jackasses. And by the way, I'm now a Muslim. Go Bruins!"

Even though no one on the team mentioned it to me or commented on it, they all knew. I was famous and if I went to a mosque or was seen in the company of other Muslims, word got around. Coach Wooden wouldn't say anything because he would have thought it was none of his business. To him, each person had to go on his or her own spiritual journey. He was probably happy that at least I was on a spiritual journey, because that meant I cared about doing the right thing. I remembered the rules he gave us the first day: "Number one in your life is your family. Number two is the religion of your choice."

Then came the night when it finally was brought in the open in front of the whole team, including Coach Wooden. That simple bus ride, like so many we had taken before, became one of the most memorable nights of my life—a night no one who was on that bus ever forgot. Bill Sweek later described it as "an iconic moment in my life and our team's life, a spiritual experience I have never forgotten." Kenny Heitz also remembered that night as special: "It's the most memorable moment of the years I spent at UCLA. It was a bunch of guys really talking, no barriers. It was just deeply special."

It was early December 1968. We had just beaten

thirteenth-ranked Ohio State in Columbus and were on our way to South Bend to play fifth-ranked Notre Dame. It was late at night, we were tired, and the bus was quiet. We weren't singing, snapping jockstraps, or drawing mustaches on sleeping teammates. For us, it was strictly a business trip. Some people were nodding off or just staring out the window at the dark fields; others were engaged in quiet discussions. I was sitting near sophomore Steve Patterson, my backup at center.

There were several different religions represented on our team that year: five or six Christians, several of them evangelicals; two Jews; and me, the only Muslim. Steve Patterson was a born-again Christian who was not reticent to talk about his beliefs. He thought that all people should be Christians if they had any hope of saving their souls and not going to hell. He wasn't being arrogant but seemed to be speaking from a heartfelt concern about the eternal lives of his teammates. He couldn't bear to think of them suffering in hell. It was clear that he had no clue about my recent conversion. The more he talked, the louder his voice became. I was only half listening as he loudly proclaimed his beliefs. I'd been hearing this stuff all my life in Catholic school.

But finally he went a little too far for me when he said,

"You know, Christ died for all men. Christ is the only salvation if you don't want to go to hell."

"Wait a second, Steve," I interrupted. "What about all those people around the world who never heard of Christ? Aren't they going to be saved?"

Steve shook his head. "No, I don't think so."

"Thanks a lot, Steve," John Ecker snorted. He was Jewish.

"Let me get this straight," I said to Steve. "Some little toddler in India dies of cholera and she goes straight to hell?"

He hesitated. "Probably purgatory."

"Why purgatory? She's just a child. She didn't do anything wrong."

"We're all born in sin, Lew," he replied.

"But she's not guilty of anything."

"We're all guilty. Because of Eve. Read your Bible, man."

"I've read it, Steve. And it doesn't make a whole lot of sense."

"It does if you *really* read it."

"I *really* read it. Which is how I know that purgatory is never mentioned in the Bible. The word isn't even used as a noun until the twelfth century."

It was the same discussion that was probably happening in a hundred dorm rooms across the country, with students just as earnest and just as sure they were in the right.

As our voices rose, other teammates turned to listen. Maybe they were hoping for a fistfight to break up the monotony of the bus ride, or maybe they were just interested in the discussion. At the front of the bus, I could see the back of Coach Wooden's head bent over whatever Western novel he was reading. Either he didn't hear us or didn't want to get involved.

Instead of escalating into a shouting match, Steve and I both switched gears and started listening. We stopped trying to be right and just tried to get to know each other's beliefs better. Other players, who were spread throughout the bus, began moving closer. Eventually, almost the entire team was gathered in the middle of the bus, leaning over the seats to participate. A few of them began voicing their own opinions. No one was attempting to simply defend his own beliefs; instead, everyone was listening and asking questions. We all opened up that night, as we drove through the dark Indiana countryside, with a trusting intimacy that we had never experienced before. Some talked about how they questioned their own faith, others how they had lost their faith. Some about how leaving home brought them closer to their faith. Never had we been closer to one another as individuals. Never had we been closer as a team. Never would we be this close again.

Which is why I suddenly felt the compulsion to say, "For those who haven't heard, I've converted to Orthodox Islam."

There was the kind of silence you might hear in deep outer space.

I braced myself for the onslaught. Now that I'd opened Pandora's box, I should expect the usual venom to follow. But it didn't. Some already knew. Those who didn't know were only mildly surprised. They knew I was studying religion, philosophy, and politics. They could see the books I always had with me on the bus trips or in the locker room: Eldridge Cleaver's *Soul on Ice*, William Barrett's *Irrational Man: A Study in Existential Philosophy*, and of course, *The Autobiography of Malcolm X*. Instead of judging me, they expressed a lively curiosity about the process that took me to that decision and what it meant to be a Muslim.

"What's the difference between Black Muslim and, uh, regular Muslim?"

"Why did Muslims kill Malcolm X if he was also a Muslim?"

Coach Wooden made his way back and joined in the conversation, but only to ask the occasional question, not to moderate or direct it. I glanced over at him a few times to see if I could gauge any reaction to my announcement, but all I saw was a wide smile of joy, not at me but at the team. His boys weren't just basketball players; they were the mature, respectful gentlemen he wanted us to be. For him, that was more important than any championship.

Coach was also worried about our afterlife. But to him that meant life after basketball. To him, basketball was a teaching tool to prepare us to live rich, fulfilling lives as fathers, husbands, and community members. And for a couple of hours that night in December, he knew he didn't have to worry about our afterlife.

37

Good-bye, Yellow Brick Road

My final year of basketball at UCLA was basically a repeat of the previous years. We won our third consecutive NCAA National Basketball Championship. I finished my college career with eighty-eight wins and only two losses. I became the only player in history to be named three-time NCAA Final Four Most Outstanding Player, and I received the first-ever Naismith Trophy presented to the country's top college player, was named Helms Foundation Player of the Year, and was chosen First Team All-American.

While I was pleased with our team's success, I was going through the same acute senioritis I'd had in my last year of high school. I was bored with what I had been doing and just wanted the next act of my life to begin. I was done with campus life, with college basketball, with still being treated as a kid with a lot of potential, who some people thought would get my butt handed to me when playing professional basketball against all those hardened veterans who knew a lot of tricks to hurt you without the referee noticing.

Bring it on, I thought.

My senior year brought several offers to play basketball professionally, but the two I was most interested in were from rival groups. The National Basketball Association (NBA) was more established, but its rivals, the upstart American Basketball Association (ABA), needed to attract big names to draw more fans. I was happy to exploit that rivalry to get the best financial offer possible. In truth, I was rooting more for the ABA, because the New York Nets were interested in me and I preferred to live in my hometown where all my friends were. The option from the NBA was the Milwaukee Bucks, which had earned the right to draft me by winning a coin toss with the Phoenix Suns.

My future was being decided by a *coin toss*!

Rather than having a long-drawn-out, back-and-forth negotiation, my adviser and I decided we would ask each team to submit one offer. We would then choose the best. Both teams agreed. First, I met with Wes Pavalon, in charge of the ownership group of the Bucks. I tried to keep my face immobile as he detailed his generous offer, which would make me a millionaire. I was only twenty-two years old and being offered more money than I had ever imagined when growing up in the projects of New York City. Maybe it was petty of me, but I couldn't help but think of all those kids who had deliberately iced me out in school, my ex–best friend Johnny yelling in my face, the old lady at the Bat Rack calling me nigger. This was serious in-your-face money.

It's a weird feeling to be offered that much money. My first thoughts were that I could finally buy a car that I didn't have to worry about breaking down. That I could travel anywhere in the world I wanted, and not have to play a basketball game when I got there. I could help out my parents so they'd never have to worry again about money.

The next morning, I met with Arthur Brown, the owner of the Nets, and Commissioner George Mikan of the ABA. I was pretty excited because I figured their offer would be even better than the one from the Bucks. I'd be even richer and I'd get to live in New York. But it turned out that their offer was much less.

My adviser, Sam Gilbert, leaned forward and said, "Is that everything? The whole package?"

"Yes," said Mikan. He looked surprised at the question,

as if he thought we would be jumping around his office in joy at his offer. "That's everything."

Sam sighed. "You understand that there is only one bid? We're not negotiating after this?"

"Understood," Mikan said. "We think we've made a generous offer that should make Lew very happy." He looked at me to see if I was "very happy."

I again tried to keep my face impassive, but I was definitely not happy.

When we got outside, I let Sam know just how surprised and unhappy I was. "What just happened in there, Sam?"

Sam shook his head. "I don't know. I expected better from them."

"Yeah, no kidding. A lot better."

Sam shrugged. "So what do you want to do?"

"I want to stay in New York," I said.

"I know, Lew. It's your decision, of course, but do you want to give up a substantially larger offer in order to stay here?"

I thought about it. I would be living on my own for the first time. No parents, no roommates. I could afford a nice apartment, but it would be a lot more fun to be near my friends, the jazz clubs, the big-city lifestyle. But I was also a little angry at the Nets for not valuing me more. If this was how they treated me when they were trying to woo me, how would they treat me once I signed a five-year contract? Five years is a long time to feel resentment.

"Milwaukee is on Lake Michigan," Sam said. "Sounds pretty."

"The name comes from the Indians," I said. "Means 'gathering place by the water.'"

He looked at me with surprise.

"I did my research," I said. "About seven hundred thousand people, a fifth of them black. They're famous for making beer. They have four of the world's largest breweries."

"See? You're practically a native already."

That afternoon we called Wes Pavalon and told him I would be joining the Milwaukee Bucks.

He seemed delighted but surprised, as if he was worried we were pranking him. "This is your final answer?"

"Yes, it's final," Sam assured him.

"This isn't a negotiating ploy to goose the Nets into offering more?"

"Nope," Sam said. "We're ready to sign and learn how to spell Milwaukee."

Pavalon laughed. "Okay, I'm counting on your word

because once I leak this to the press, there will be a lot of reaction."

"Draw up the papers," Sam said. "And bring your checkbook." He hung up the phone and looked at me. "You are now a Wisconsinite. What do they call them?"

"Cheeseheads," I said. "It's known as 'America's Dairyland.'"

He grabbed his belly and grinned. "This is mostly thanks to cheese and beer, so I'll be right at home when I visit you."

That evening, the news of my joining the Bucks was all over the television. I was in my room trying to stay away from reporters when I heard frantic knocking on my hotel door. It was Sam. He rushed in, his face red with anger.

"You are not going to believe what just happened!" he said.

"What?" I said.

He took a deep breath, calming himself. "I just got stopped in the hotel lobby by two ABA owners. They want to increase their offer."

I didn't say anything. I didn't know what to say.

"I explained that they had agreed to a one-time bid, but they said Mikan didn't have the authority to make a final offer. They want us to hold off signing with the Bucks."

"What's their offer?"

He told me. It was three times higher than the Bucks'.

I sat down on the bed, a little dazed. It was more than I had even hoped for at our meeting.

A long silence hung in the room like a cold mist.

"What do you want to do, Lew?" Sam asked.

Lew knew what he wanted to do: Take the money and run. But it wasn't Lew who answered, it was Kareem Abdul-Jabbar. Kareem had learned in the mosque to be truthful and honest in all dealings. True, I had learned the same teachings in the Roman Catholic Church, but I had chosen Islam as my spiritual path and couldn't abandon it the first time I was faced with temptation.

"I gave my word, Sam," I said. "I'm a Cheesehead."

He looked me in the eyes, and I could see the pride in his expression. "Yeah, you are," he said, a slight catch in his voice.

38

Becoming Kareem— For Real

What's it like to play professional basketball?

Two words: Very. Hard.

I thought the transition from college player to pro would be a lot easier than it was. But I didn't take into consideration the fact that I would be living alone. In a city far away from all my friends and family. In a place that got colder than anything I'd ever experienced. A place with no active Muslim community. Yes, I was a famous athlete making lots of money, but when I wasn't on the basketball court with my teammates, I mostly felt lonely. I had the massive phone bills to prove it.

I struggled to maintain my focus on Islam, which prohibited gambling, alcohol, and casual dating. I wanted to be as pious as possible, but loneliness ate away at my resolve. I still avoided gambling and alcohol, but I allowed myself to date women I wasn't serious about, just to ease the isolation. I still hadn't made my conversion or my new name public, but I didn't keep it a secret from my teammates. One player, Don Smith, just couldn't understand why I had done it.

"What is Islam exactly?" he asked.

I'd been through this enough to have my fortune cookie–sized answer ready: "Basically, we believe there is only one god, Allah, and that his last messenger was Muhammad."

That wasn't enough for Don. "Yeah, but what's the message that Muhammad brought?"

He seemed sincere, not challenging, so I continued. "There are five basic rules, called the Five Pillars: faith, prayer, charity, fasting, and a pilgrimage to Mecca."

"Sounds simple enough."

"Well," I said, "it's not *that* simple. Like they say, God is in the details."

We didn't discuss those details. He seemed more interested in why I asked guests to remove their shoes when entering my house. "It's Wisconsin, man!" he complained. "We could freeze to death." A few years later, after he was traded to Houston, Don converted to Islam and became Zaid Abdul-Aziz.

The fans and players in Milwaukee couldn't have been nicer. When I arrived that first day of rookie camp, I walked onto the court and received a three-minute standing ovation. They were all pinning their hopes on me to help pull the team up from its previous season, when it lost more than two-thirds of its games. I felt the pressure immediately, as if a heavy saddle had been thrown onto my back. But at the same time, I was exhilarated by the challenge and by the goodwill of my teammates and the Milwaukee community. I wanted to do well for them.

A big difference between college and pro basketball is the grueling schedule. In college, we played twice a week, and we played for college pride as much as we played for ourselves. In the pros, we played as often as four times a week, with little time or energy left over to work up civic pride. Fortunately, Coach Wooden's endless running drills had physically prepared me for the pace. I was still running full speed down the court when the rest of the rookies were panting in a slow jog.

Another difference was how much more physical the players were. I was grabbed, held, elbowed, and kneed, mostly without any calls from the refs. It was the Big Man Paradox. Because I was taller than most other players, it was assumed that I could take more abuse as a way to even things out. However, if I tried to defend myself with the same level of physicality, I received a foul.

I quickly learned how to adapt. I worked harder on defense, blocking shots and keeping players from getting easy shots close to the basket. They had to work harder for their shots, which meant they missed more of them. On offense, I just focused on using my speed and agility to outmaneuver them. It worked, because I was averaging twenty-eight points a game. We finished the season with a 56–26 record, good enough to give us second place in the Eastern Division. We then played our way to the Eastern Division Finals, where we lost. At the end of the season, I was awarded NBA Rookie of the Year, NBA All-Rookie Team, and NBA All-Star Game Appearance. Not bad for my first year.

The following year we acquired one of the greatest players I had ever seen, Oscar Robertson. He elevated my game and everyone else's on the team. We ended that year with a 66–16 record, including a twenty-game winning streak, which was the longest in NBA history at the time. We won the NBA Finals against Baltimore, 4–0. The Bucks had been in existence for only three years, and we were already the NBA champions. During that season, I scored 2,599 points, nearly a thousand more than the next player on our team. I was honored as the NBA Scoring Champion, NBA Most Valuable Player, and the NBA Finals Most Valuable Player.

A couple of months after we became NBA champions, I legally changed my name to Kareem Abdul-Jabbar. Until then, I hadn't been ready because I felt I hadn't yet earned the right. All my life, I had allowed others to name me, and even when they had done so with my permission and encouragement, I still had the feeling I was letting others decide who I was. This time, though, I had fought my way past all those who had doubted me, and while I appreciated all my coaches and teachers, I had fought beyond them, too, to stand on my own and say, "I named myself. This is the man I choose to be, not the man the world expects me to be."

Lew Alcindor, who had won all those championships and all those awards and honors, was gone forever.

Now there was just Kareem.

And now the world would see just who Kareem is and what he could do.

And I Lived Happily, Sadly, Magnificently, Boringly, Piously, Crazily Ever After

The road from Lew Alcindor to Kareem Abdul-Jabbar was dangerously twisting, overgrown with thick, thorny weeds, pocked with craters of muddy water, and filled with snakes. Lots of hidden snakes. It reminds me of the Robert Frost poem I read in college, "The Road Not Taken": "Two roads diverged in a wood, and I— / I took the one less traveled by, / And that has made all the difference."

After becoming Kareem, I went on to accomplish many things: I had a wonderful basketball career during which I set many records, some of which still stand. I became a husband and a father. I publicly fought against social injustices. I wrote articles and books. I coached high school kids and professionals. I became a US global cultural ambassador. I received the Presidential Medal of Freedom from President Obama.

I also made many, many mistakes on that road. I tried hard to be a good friend, a good father, a good husband, a good Muslim, and a good American. I wish I had done a better job with each of those. I'm not sad about that, though, because I realized that "becoming Kareem" is not a goal but a long journey that never ends. I am always in the act of becoming Kareem—the Kareem I want to be, who is the kindest, gentlest, smartest, lovingest version of me. Today I am still trying to become Kareem. Tomorrow I will still be trying to become Kareem.

Along the way, I had many coaches, both on the court and off the court. Some, like Coach Donahue and Hamaas, I broke with to go my own way. Some, like Bruce Lee and Muhammad Ali, died while still my valued coaches. And some, like Coach Wooden, I grew closer to over the years until he became a second father to me. I am grateful to each for guiding me along the treacherous path for however long or short a time our relationship lasted. Without them, I wouldn't have finally been able to walk that path on my own, confident in my own choices. And more important, to help others along their chosen paths.

It's that last part that most interests me now: helping others along their chosen paths. That's why I wrote this book. To be that coach who takes by the hand anyone who ever feels picked on or put upon, outraged but out of range, vilified yet voiceless. Perhaps this road is not that much "less traveled by" as we think. It just seems that way because so often we feel like we're walking it alone.

I didn't walk it alone, even when I thought I was. No one has to. Coaches and teachers and family and friends are everywhere, reaching out a hand for you to take. I hope this book is one such hand.

About the Author

KAREEM ABDUL-JABBAR is the NBA's all-time leading scorer and a Basketball Hall of Fame inductee. Since retiring, he has been an actor and a basketball coach and has written many *New York Times* bestsellers. Abdul-Jabbar is also a columnist for many news outlets, such as the *Washington Post*, the *New York Times*, *Time* magazine, and the *Hollywood Reporter*, writing on a wide range of subjects including race, politics, age, and pop culture. In 2012 Abdul-Jabbar was selected as a US global cultural ambassador, and in 2016 he was awarded the Presidential Medal of Freedom, the nation's highest civilian award, which recognizes exceptional meritorious service. He lives in Southern California.